PRAISE FOR SOLE TO SOUL

"In *Sole to Soul*, Melissa Evans takes an insightful approach to inspiring and challenging you to be the best you can be. She helps you to hone your vision and use your unique skills and gifts to pursue your dreams—and reach your destiny. *Sole to Soul* is a must-read for anyone who wants to understand and capitalize on their supreme purpose in life."

— Tracy Barbour, M.S.M., CeM/Founder & CEO, RightResponse eMarketing

"*Sole to Soul* is a powerful book that helps you zero in on what makes you uniquely special and translate that uniqueness into doing work that is most meaningful and purposeful for *you*."

— Sheri Varela, Author of *Affirmations with Attitude: Sassy Power Starters to Ignite Your Day*

"If you are struggling to find and live your Soul Purpose, Melissa Evans has a gift for you—a roadmap to your future! Because she has discovered and is successfully living her own Soul Purpose, she can show you how to live yours. She offers a unique blend of inspiration and practical steps to live your life and purpose to the fullest. You need a map to create the future you want to live, and Melissa Evans has laid it out for you in this book. Get it and get going!"

— Adele Michal, MA, CreateMoreNow.com

"Melissa Evans is a woman who is concise, clear, and confident with a heart of golden warmth and wisdom. She comes from the soul, and her book *Sole to Soul* is destined to powerfully and positively impact the lives of those who are searching for their purpose within the context of their businesses *and* their personal lives. *Sole to Soul* fulfilled my soul's need for wisdom and my pragmatic need for practical life application. Loved it!"

— Valencia Ray, MD, Author of *Empower Up and Play Big*

"If you want a life living your soul purpose, living your vision, and achieving success, let Melissa Evans, the Guru of Implementation, be your guide. This book will inspire you to be the best you can be."

— AC Masiddo, CEO, SlashMedBillsandSave.com

"As a successful businesswoman that has been in business for over 30 years and served over 5,000 entrepreneurs and business owners in 239 different industries, I know the importance of being clear about what your purpose is and certain about who you are here to serve. Melissa Evans, The Guru of Implementation, is the REAL DEAL. Her book, *Sole to Soul: How to Identify your Soul Purpose and Monetize It* is filled with practical reasoning and guidance on how to live your life, serve others, and get paid handsomely for being of the upmost service. There aren't many books that can capture your attention and give you the most useful information you've ever read. This book is destined to become an instant classic!'"

— Terri Levine, Ph.D., MCC, PCC, MS, CCC-SLP
Business Growth Guru

"*Sole to Soul: How to Identify your Soul Purpose and Monetize It* is an authentic read that opens up your mind's eye and guides you through the pages on achieving personal (spiritual) and financial success."

— Michelle Christie, Founder, Motivators and Creators (MACs)

"If you have ever had an inkling to spread your wings but discarded it or have already lifted off but desire to fly higher, devour this book. Melissa Evans has distilled a powerful potion that inevitably will give you the inspiration, strength, and guidance to be forever propelled by your soul purpose."

— Sabine Messner, Soul Purpose Catalyst & Brand Visionary, EnlightenedBranding.com

"After reading Melissa Evans' new book, I am so motivated to start following my dream, not trying to accommodate others by placing my desires on the back burner. The Joel Barker quote found in Melissa's book states, 'Vision without action is a dream. Action without vision is simply passing the time. Action with vision is making a positive difference.' My plans will come to fruition by putting my vision into action.

Every person is unique (fingerprint), and one thing I have come to realize is changing yourself to win others never works for an extended period of time. You must be yourself (soul purpose); things and others will gravitate towards you when authenticity is in place."

— Mildretta Hughes, MP Hughes Educational Consulting Services

"Your thoughts and advice ring true. They are simple to the point of being near self-evident, yet no one takes the time to make people think through the aspects of their business and personal lives through these goggles of simplicity. You help us to realize that what is truly satisfying to a person in the end is feeling that our lives are meaningful and important. We can't do that living under a false ID or failing to fully realize God-given gifts."

— Nicole Kelly, Esq., President, Nia Entertainment Group Founder, Isaac's Powerhouse

"I was really inspired by the imagery using fingerprints to illustrate one's unique perspective. When I was young, my grandmother always told me to be yourself and good things will happen to you. The take away is that sometimes you have to support or challenge things that you feel are not right by taking a stance based on your morals, values, and principles. It takes courage to present a unique position that others do not feel is the corporate line."

— Jim Francis, Director, Enterprise Strategy and Architecture, CHS

"Melissa has the unique ability to motivate beyond what you think you're capable of. She uses real language combined with practical, real world advice. She's steeped in brilliant business sense and has taught me the true meaning of soul purpose living without me having to believe in a specific higher power."

— Jimbo Marshall, Owner, YourVideoSolution.com

"In *Sole to Soul*, the reader gets to see what it looks like to live and work according to one's soul purpose. With her illuminating discussion of the soul's 'fingerprint,' Melissa urges us to be ourselves and express our innate gifts. She consistently grounds her premises with strategies designed to help us bring out our uniqueness and make our vision real. What starts out as a possibility—the idea of living according to your soul purpose—ends up being more of a probability if we apply Melissa's engaging principles and methods!"

— Deborah Lindholm, MACP, Relationship Mentor & Inner Power Expert, SerenityMatters.com

"As we claim our uniqueness in our business and personal lives, we're served when we attend to the details of creating a clear vision to express our uniqueness, and Melissa Evans shares 10 principles for how to do just that!"

— Kit Furey, JD, CHt, CEHP, WholeMindMaster.com

"Inspiring! Melissa Evans guides the reader to discover or even *re-discover* their unique essence of purpose, vision, and self-appreciation. The transformation is inevitable and real! Once you finish this book, look up and look ahead—you'll see no limits!"

— Steve Cozart, President, Dynamic Appeal Communications

"Getting clear on my big vision and achieving it is a constant challenge for me. I've read dozens of books, hired coaches for thousands of dollars, and gone to many, many workshops and seminars on creating your vision. Melissa's approach is different because not only does she guide you through setting your vision, but then she goes on to talk about how to actually live your vision! I'm excited because this is the missing piece of the puzzle in everything I've learned."

— Erin Ferree, Brand Stylist and Strategist, BrandStyle Design

"As a publicist I have seen many authors over the years discuss the issues of inspiration, purpose, and happiness. Finally an author presents a practical and clear concept on these areas that matter so much to all of us. Melissa Evans provides an inspirational and practical roadmap to realizing who we are and how to turn that knowledge into something meaningful. This book will be on my nightstand for years to come!"

— Anne Leedom, Founder, Net Connect Publicity

"I have always known I was different. *Sole to Soul* helps validate things I knew to be true for me, but never really understood. Reading about my 'unique fingerprint' gives me the permission to fully embrace my 'one of a kindness' and relish knowing that it is this that allows me to carve out my own path and serve in a way that is distinct and unique to me."

— Natalie Jobity, President of Elan Image Management, Author of *Frumpy to Fabulous: Flaunting It*

"While devouring *Sole to Soul,* I felt as if Melissa Evans was speaking directly to me, as if she wrote the book specifically for me. My favorite part was learning about my own unique fingerprint and how unique and special I am. I don't have to be anybody but ME in order to live my dream and fulfill my purpose. Understanding the depth and knowledge that uniquely identifies me allows me to go out in this world, speak my truth, shine my light bright, and be unapologetically ME."

— Melissa Risdon

"You have touched the heart of my passion with your new book. It is vital that we find and live our Soul's purpose, identify and be our unique 'Fingerprint.' I am impressed, but not surprised, by your masterful writing on this roadmap to a successful life."

— Les Schmidt, Author, Speaker, Coach, FindingYourOwnTruth.com

"*Sole to Soul* is a book that is so needed today. If you are up to making a difference in your life, being successful, and having fun doing it, this is a must-read. Melissa has a way of inspiring you with the passion, clarity, humor, and humanity we all need to remind ourselves of when we go forth and express our soul purpose in the world. Her insightful teaching about our own personal fingerprint as our soul source is powerful, heart opening, and leaves you totally inspired to go forth and express your divine unique fingerprint for everyone to experience and enjoy. Melissa provides deep inspiration with plenty of real life how-to's that will have you on your way to success and fun with your soul's purpose!"

— Joy Perreras, Creator & Mentor, RelaxingIntoSuccess.com

"Melissa Evans shares practical advice for those who want to fully live their vision and purpose. You will find *Sole to Soul* insightful."

— Kimber Britner, President of Moxie Me Institute, MoxieMe.com

"*Sole to Soul* touched my soul in a way that was inspirational, actionable, and extremely enjoyable. Melissa weaves practical strategies with specific metaphors for how each of us truly makes a difference in the world by believing in our own uniqueness. Nice work!"

— Skip Weisman, The Leadership & Workplace Communication Expert, WorkplaceCommunicationExpert.com

"Unlike traditional authors who give advice without truly living it themselves, Melissa Evans is the strongest type of woman whose words come off the page and hit you in your soul. She sparkles by building a theory of finding, and then following the calling your soul WANTS to live. She helps develop content, skills, and reminders that will ensure true direction. Evans' concepts are based on belief systems and positive associations which she calls 'Tribes.' Her comprehensive, personalized strategies help foster profound improvements in the reader's quality of life. Evans is able to share information and life skills with the reader that can't be taught in any school. Her writings construct self-esteem by answering the call the soul has dialed."

— Tammy Valentic, Senior Project Manager, a Leading National Healthcare Company

"Melissa's brilliant Fingerprint Model reminded me to embrace the comfortable knowing of my unique self so I could make room for my deeper soul vision. Her easy to implement tools made it simple to re-align my life's mission. This book is a key resource in my purpose-driven library."

— Stacey Canfield, Artist, Photographer, Author of *The Soul Sitter: A New Vision for Soul Care for the Dying and the Inspiring Story of the Woman Behind It.*

"I think deep down inside we all know what our purpose is—what it is that we are meant to do. It just takes some longer to realize that purpose than others. *Sole to Soul: How to Identify Your Soul Purpose and Monetize It* can help you realize that purpose more quickly than if you were to do it on your own. The book provides guidance on not only determining what you feel is your purpose, but also the steps to take so that you can turn a vision into an action. I know from owning my own business and working 70+ hours a week at times that your vision can be attained, but I also know that it can take on a life of its own. I definitely recommend this book to anyone that has always had a vision of where they see themselves in life and want to not only capitalize on that vision, but also live their true purpose, as that is what attaining true happiness and success is all about."

— Valerie Mellema, Co-Founder, WordsYouWant.com

SOLE TO SOUL

SOLE TO SOUL

How to Identify Your Soul
Purpose and Monetize It

MELISSA EVANS

Sole to Soul

By Melissa Evans

DEDICATION

To my daddy, who, with all of his imperfections,

accepted me with all my imperfections.

The influence of his soul purpose lives on,

even though he is gone.

CONTENTS

FOREWORD

In today's fast-paced, cutthroat world, many entrepreneurs feel like they have to sell their soul to live in abundance. They believe that in order to reach ultimate success, they have to give up who they are—and when they finally get there, they feel like they are unfulfilled.

Well, I have news for you (and it's good news)—only YOU can be the best at being you. That's why only you can fulfill what author Melissa Evans calls "your Soul Purpose."

When you come to appreciate and understand this concept, you can make money and live well, unapologetically, simply by being yourself.

How do I know this is true? Because I lived it and I grew a multi-million-dollar home-based business in three years with no employees and two toddlers in tow.

I was able to do this because I was building a business around my soul purpose—being the Queen of Sales Conversion—and helping other heart-based entrepreneurs and agents of change get their message out into the world in a big way and being paid handsomely for it.

This book is a no-nonsense, practical guide to monetizing your soul purpose by honoring your soul and serving your tribe, two things that combine to create a life filled with harmony, abundance, and personal fulfillment.

What makes *Sole to Soul: How to Identify Your Soul Purpose and Monetize It* differently from other business-building books on the shelves today? Sure, *Sole to Soul* talks about business. But it talks about creating a thriving business as it relates to being of the utmost service, feeding your soul and being who you are.

Just as importantly, it provides timely and timeless advice you can use now to take action and create a life of service and abundance—a life you love—by living your soul purpose.

So, if you're struggling in your life and wondering why things just aren't going your way, or if you're making great money, but feel like something is still missing in your life, or if you crave developing million-dollar status and using it to serve your community, keep this book on your nightstand.

Melissa Evans, a heart-centered businesswoman who was a self-made millionaire by 31, writes (and writes well) about what she does best—creating a plan that drives maximum revenue and provides maximum service. She's known as The Guru of Implementation, and that's because she has a proven track record for helping corporations, entrepreneurs, and individuals achieve abundance through Soul Purpose Implementation.

Melissa has created—and you hold in your hands—*the* must-have guide for taking the shortest and most direct path to living your best, most fulfilled life while serving your community, simply by being yourself.

— Lisa Sasevich, The Queen of Sales Conversion

ACKNOWLEDGEMENTS

MY CONVERSATION WITH GOD, I have to acknowledge…

Your soul purpose is to bring joy to people's souls.

*Well God, you have told me this for a while now.
How do I do this?*

**Share your talents with the world. Show them there is never a
bad day. Every day and moment is divine.**

I understand that, but what does that blessing look like?

**It looks like your life. Nothing has been in vain; your pain has
been your transformation. You were never alone; I had you the
whole time. Remember when you felt the most love?**

*Yes, God, I felt the most love when I no longer had any material
things, and I looked around and saw everyone that was still left.*

And who else did you finally see?

You

God is in everything. Understand that, and joy
will always be in your soul.

God = Love

Tap into divine love, and your abundance will be
overwhelming, materially and spiritually.

Very special thanks to Lisa Sasevich, The Queen of Conversion, for writing the foreword of my book.

Very special thanks to Mia Redrick, my book coach, who allowed me to get the words that have been embedded in my heart out into the universe.

Very special thanks to Stacey Canfield of www.myimageartist.com for my photos. Also, Natalie Jobity – Image Diva, Lauren Clark – Make Up and Hair on Set, and Merlene Crews – Hair for helping me to present my best look in the photos.

Very special thanks to my mom, Dr. Verna Benjamin-Lambert, who has been a great example for me. She taught me not to accept any limitations, and it is because of her and her level of standards and excellence that have made me who I am today.

To my family Harry, Nicole, Nadia, Lauren, and extended family, who all played a significant role in my development, my perspective, and my ultimate self-acceptance, I am forever grateful.

To my father, the late Errol Evans, who played a strong role in allowing me to just BE.

To Angelo Hughes, my silent strength and partner.

To Kimberly Lockett Criswell, my soul protector.

And to those of you who are a part of my family and growing circle of friends, thank you for being such an amazing support system, even if you didn't know it—I am forever grateful.

SECTION ONE

INSPIRING SUCCESS:
SOUL PURPOSE LIVING

THE FIRST SECTION OF THIS book is intended to provide a safe place for you, the reader, to explore what soul purpose living means to you, out loud. Discovering your soul purpose is a journey that begins with a close look at what inspires you and then delves deeper to discover the inspiration and beauty you already have within you.

Soul purpose living is all about love.

It's a journey that's well worth taking, and the contents of the chapters are designed to demonstrate that wherever you are destined to go in life, you already have everything you need to get you there, and whoever you are destined to be in life, you already have the gifts you need to be that person.

Everyone has ups and downs in life, and it's my intention that you will be able to use this section to reflect on your own life experiences and, in the process, reconnect with the real you and the things that provide you with the most love. It's an opportunity to discover the things that matter most to you in life and perhaps rediscover the things you feel most passionate about.

To live your soul purpose fully means to discover who you really are and to accept yourself as you really are. As you read through these chapters, you will learn the true value of just being yourself and how just being you, no matter how quirky that may seem to others, is all you need to do to be successful in life.

Some of you may have reached a point in your lives where you know there's something missing, and you know you have something more to give. You're just not sure what that something is. The contents of this section will help you to find that missing something and point you in the right direction to begin living a life of fulfillment. We each have our own unique gifts to offer the world, but, often, the value of those gifts has gone unrecognized or forgotten along the way.

Some of you may already have identified your soul purpose and now need confirmation and support to grow more confident in that purpose. These chapters will help you to develop a clearer understanding of what soul purpose living really is and guide you through the process of stepping up into your purpose and sharing your gift with the world.

**Every one of us has a soul,
and every one of us already has a soul purpose:
enjoy your voyage of discovery.**

CHAPTER ONE
BE INSPIRED

**When you live your soul purpose,
you are unstoppable.**

TO LIVE YOUR SOUL PURPOSE, you must know what your purpose is—so how do you know? The best place to begin your search is inside yourself. The answer is rarely found externally, although there may be an external trigger that prompts you to search internally. *You* have that answer. It shows up in the things you typically do, but finding it depends on how ready you are to receive it.

Discovering your purpose is a journey, but it's also a discovery that can unearth an enormous source of strength you may not know that you own. Self-love, self-acceptance, and an acceptance of your gifts give you an inner confidence. Whatever the world throws at you, you are secure in the knowledge that you are loved, and the power of that love surrounds you like a virtual suit of armour. You know there's nothing that anyone can ever say or do that can take your gifts away. Your gifts have been given to *you*, and they will lead you to your own source of inspiration which, in turn, will bring an understanding of what feeds your soul and what you need to do to live your purpose.

The journey to your purpose is traveling through the process of knowing yourself, loving yourself, and being yourself.

KNOW YOURSELF · LOVE YOURSELF · BE YOURSELF

"Your time is limited, so don't waste it living someone else's life. Don't be trapped by dogma, which is living with the results of other people's thinking. Don't let the noise of others' opinions drown out your own inner voice. And most important, have the courage to follow your heart and intuition. They somehow already know what you truly want to become. Everything else is secondary."
—Steve Jobs, Apple co-founder

KNOW YOURSELF

I was an intensely curious child who always asked a lot of questions. My natural curiosity was not valued or recognized as a gift in my childhood. In fact, it was actively discouraged by my authority figures from as early as I can remember. I always found it difficult to take things at face value or accept limitations. I never fit into a tidy box and was never good at adhering to standards that I did not understand. I naturally rejected the status quo before I knew what status quo meant. This tendency made me unpopular among some. I never felt accepted and never fit in. Even proceeding with the best of intentions did not exempt me from the negative feelings that often seemed to develop in others toward me anytime I sought merely to follow up on a desire to know the most I could about the world around me.

Later in life, I realized that the same curiosity that seemed to plague my existence in youth translated into a most marketable skill when I arrived in the working world. In the corporate world, I found my context—a place where my natural tendencies were relevant and valued. My naturally scrutinizing mind allowed me to view corporate challenges in a way that brought people of varying perspectives together. What previously made me an eccentric elevated me to change agent status, armed with the ability to ignite a corporate change process that diffused fear about change and inspire many corporate stakeholders to take an active role in utilizing their individual values to add to the corporate bottom line. I am now regularly tasked with bringing order to chaos, utilizing the very same skills that labeled me as rebellious and unmanageable in my early years.

Once I learned to look at my natural tendencies as possibilities rather than limitations, my horizons were necessarily expanded. Once I saw myself as having a unique and indelible fingerprint on the world, I opened up my own possibilities. This process of self-knowledge is not one that occurs overnight, nor is it one that always happens as easily and readily as we would like, but the effort is worthwhile and doable. There are some definitive steps you can take to arriving at a place of self-knowing. It can take some time to recognize your own fingerprint and understand its context and value.

Getting to a point in your life where you can recognize the value of your natural gifts is a journey, and it's important to recognize that the journey, in itself, has a value. Not being able to find *instant* answers doesn't mean you can't ever find them. It can take time to recognize your own gifts and to understand their value, especially if you are discouraged from doing or using what comes naturally to you in childhood. However, by learning to love your natural self, the *real* you, you learn to recognize what comes naturally to you, and you also learn to recognize what inspires you.

Along with self-acceptance
comes an acceptance of your gifts.

Recognizing your gifts is only the beginning. You must then accept them as yours. Your gift may be something that makes you stand out from the crowd. Perhaps you are gifted physically and have an above-average athletic ability. Perhaps you are gifted academically and have an above-average ability in math or spelling, but *not* standing out from the crowd does not mean you are not gifted. It's quite possible that your gifts have gone unrecognized by you because they are the things that come naturally to you, while others may have wondered at your talents and asked, "How do you do that?"

FINDING YOUR FINGERPRINT

Take time to identify the times in your life when you have felt the most capable, happy, and fulfilled. Identifying yourself is, in part, knowing what naturally makes you tick and what always gets in your way. Start by asking yourself the following questions:

- What are your personal strengths?
- What are your professional strengths?
- What skills come easily to you?
- When in your life have you felt the most successful?
- Whose story or circumstance has moved you to tears?
- What fills you up with joy?
- At what point or time in your life have you felt (or do you feel) most at peace?
- What life situations make you feel immediately outside of your comfort zone?
- What do you look forward to, and what do you dread?

While the above inquiries won't necessarily uncover everything you need to know on your journey to self-discovery, they will give you some insights into where you are headed. One thing is for certain: By simply raising your awareness about your life experiences and how they affect you, you will become better at knowing what fits and doesn't fit with your most natural and comfortable definition of self.

LOVE YOURSELF

What you love is a sign from your higher self
of what you are to do."
–Sanaya Roman

Once you find your fingerprint, you will be amazed at how many of life's instances were evidence of your personal brand. You may also be surprised to see the many patterns of similar behavior and viewpoints that you have had in the past that have been consistent with your identified fingerprint, often without your having ever defined for yourself what makes you unique. For me, the path to truly loving myself was through my relationship with God. The love of God led the way to my loving and accepting myself for who I really am. I know that in God's eyes, I am perfect just as I am. My belief in his perfection and his divine decision to create me taught me to love me as I believe that he does. As a result of my relationship with God, I no longer need to please others to find acceptance or love.

BE YOURSELF

"The most terrifying thing is to accept oneself completely."
–Carl Jung

It took a journey of over thirty years for me to realize the importance of just being me. Once you embark on the course of finding out who you really are, it usually unearths another challenge on the journey to soul purpose. How do you take this person you have discovered you are and allow that person to live comfortably and undisturbed in your own skin? How do you reconcile, now that you have identified who you are, the person you are with the person you have become under the influence of others? How can you learn how to "just be"? Learning to just be means learning to recognize the real you, the person you know yourself to be internally, not the person you may have become in order to "fit in" or please others. Learning to just be is the process of engaging in life's moments in a state of elevated consciousness as you remain on the alert for the purpose of your own actions. It means making yourself undergo an ongoing analysis of whether your actions truly fit in with who you know yourself to be. When you learn to just be, you learn to trust your inner self, and you learn to love your true self.

SOUL PURPOSE

So you know what moves you, you embrace who you are, you are comfortable in your own skin, and you are ready to use your natural gifts to carve out a fulfilled life. What is your soul purpose? Finding the answer to that begins with an understanding of where to look.

YOUR SOUL PURPOSE IS INSPIRED.

Soul purpose is a by-product of living committed to your natural gifts. Inspiration draws us nearer to which actions represent committed living in our personal and professional lives. For me, inspiration is divine, and my source is God. Inspiration for others may come from spiritual sources or from nature. Meditation practices can encourage a deeper connection with your true self, leading to opportunities to recognize and value your gifts. Getting back to nature or simply spending quiet time away from the distractions of everyday life can also provide opportunities to connect with your inner self and find inspiration. Whatever the source, *your* inspiration comes from within *you*.

Inspiration comes from a place of love. Where you love and who you love matter.

Establishing Inspirational Environments and Circumstances

There's an unquestionable connection between your environment and your source of inspiration. When you find the right environment for you, you feed your soul, and knowing what feeds your soul is a key component of soul purpose living. The world around you is often a mirror of who you are. It will always be easier to find inspiration in an environment that feeds your soul, so it becomes important to be able to recognize that environment.

What environment allows you to laugh and/or feel joy?

Where do you feel most at home and most comfortable? In the city? In a rural setting? Near water? What environments are you naturally drawn to? Identifying the environmental elements that are most inspirational for you makes it possible to bring those elements into your everyday world. For example, if you live in a land-locked area, but you discover you feel naturally drawn to water, consider installing a small indoor waterfall in your home or playing music recordings that bring the sounds of water and nature into your home.

Cultivating Inspirational Relationships

Have you ever been around someone who makes you feel like you can accomplish anything? Have you been around someone whose presence drains your inspiration? If you have ever been in either of these circumstances, you know the impact that the company you keep can have on your ability to fulfill your soul purpose. No inspiration, no soul purpose. Your inspiration does not depend on others, but there is no faster way to snuff it out than by including uninspired and negative people in your circle of daily experience.

As the seasoned gardener knows that a removal of weeds and trimming back of old branches are required for new stems to develop and flourish, so we must learn that if we expect progress. You will never ultimately be able to avoid all of these people, but it is possible to limit your exposure to them.

SOUL PURPOSE IN ACTION: SOLE PURPOSE

What is sole purpose? Sole purpose is what results in the business world when a business is conducted by a person or collective operating in its soul purpose. It, in fact, involves identical steps. Know your business, love your business, be your business. Identify your greater service (business gift), live in your greatest service to your sole purpose. While fulfilling our soul purpose is the recipe for a greater sense of happiness and contentedness in our personal lives, defining and fulfilling our sole purpose through our life's work is the key to professional success and monetizing our natural talents. Incidentally, sole purpose is also our key to leaving an indelible fingerprint on the world around us that will last long after we have departed this earth.

Inspired Universal Gifts

Walt Disney was an inspired businessman. His vision was to build a magical place where adults and children could have fun together. His unique creative gifts became gifts to the universe.

> *"Disneyland is a work of love. We didn't go into
> Disneyland just with the idea of making money."*
> – Walt Disney

In 1886 the curiosity of John Pemberton led to the creation of the now globally recognized drink, Coca-Cola®. As the business grew and the brand developed, an inspired purpose evolved.

Company Mission:
- To refresh the world in mind, body, and spirit.
- To inspire moments of optimism through our brands and actions.
- To create value and make a difference everywhere we engage.

"Don't undermine your worth by comparing yourself with others. It is because we are different that each of us is special."
– Bryan Dyson, CEO, Coca-Cola

Your gifts are unique to you, and you are a unique fingerprint in the world. No one can be better at being you than you. Your soul purpose is inspired, and no one can do what you are inspired to do better than you. The same goes for your soul-inspired business. I believe that your business purpose can create ripples after your physical departure. If I live my soul purpose, then the people I come into contact with will allow a piece of me to live on inside of them. A successfully operating business necessarily expands beyond your personal reach. As such, its potential territory is far more expansive. The following pneumonic device can assist in your understanding of how personal soul purpose relates to business sole purpose:

Individuals and Small Companies
S - sales and support
O - operations and delivery / soul purpose implementation
U - unique marketing strategy
L - leverage your talents / gifts

Bigger Companies and Big Business
S - systems that are repeatable / streamlined and support change management
O - one purpose / one goal
L - leadership, advisement, and coaching
E - enterprise-wide implementation / sole purpose implementation

When a corporation becomes totally focused on how it can be of the utmost service, it becomes focused on fulfilling its **sole** purpose. Providing the utmost service as a company means providing the utmost service to each individual who buys the product or uses the service provided by the company. For example, when Bill Gates founded Microsoft, his **sole** purpose was to place a personal computer in every household in the world. His **sole** purpose was also his **soul** purpose, as he recognized that personal computers would enhance the lives of people who had one in their home. He understood the value of his gift, not only because of what he stood to gain, personally, but also because of the potential it created for others to gain. Through him, his gift became a gift to the universe.

How does a company know that it is operating in its sole purpose?

- The customers understand the company's vision.
- Sales goals are met.
- The company is forward-moving, and the business structure is agile.
- The leadership empowers staff members.
- Repeat customers.
- Operations are streamlined, timely, and within budget.
- The culture is healthy.
- People enjoy coming to work.
- People are motivated to be productive, and direction is clear.
- People are held accountable to goals that support the overall company goals.
- Staff is encouraged to bring ideas to leadership and to be innovative problem solvers.
- The environment is ethical.
- The overall corporate vision and purpose are clear.
- The right employees are given the right tools at the right time.

How does a company know that it has not found its sole purpose?

- People hate coming to work.
- Sales are not predictable, and goals are not being met.
- Marketing efforts are unsuccessful.
- Delivery of goods/services is not efficient, deadlines are missed, and budget overruns are commonplace.
- Appropriate resources are not available to accomplish goals:
- Lack of skilled staff.
- Appropriate tools not provided to skilled staff.
- Lack of accountability, direction, and vision.
- Lack of leadership.
- Lack of sound decisions being made to support corporate goals.
- Too many turf wars that hinder corporate progress.
- Disablement of highly productive workers.
- Mediocrity is celebrated.
- The status quo is ingrained culturally.
- Unethical environment.
- High turnover.
- Frequent absenteeism.

When a company becomes totally focused on how it can be of the utmost service, it becomes focused on fulfilling its **sole** purpose. Evidence of this is business success and longevity.

CHAPTER TWO
STAND IN YOUR PURPOSE, DON'T SIT

"Our true identity is love without fear and insecurity.
Our higher potential finds us when we set our course
in that direction. The power of love and compassion
transforms insecurity."
—Doc Childre

YOUR SOUL PURPOSE IS INSPIRED. Once you get it, what are you going to do with it? Are you going to stand or sit in it? If you're standing in your purpose, you have not only recognized what your purpose is, you have taken ownership of it and have begun to live your life in a way that will allow you to fulfill it. You have accepted who you are, and you have accepted the gifts you have been given. When you're standing firmly in your purpose, you become strong like a tree firmly rooted in place; you become hard to knock down.

You know you're standing in your purpose when...

...you feel driven, focused, unafraid, and secure in an undeniable belief that you are destined to do whatever it is that you do.

...you experience a sense of urgency, but also an abundance of energy when you do what you do to live your purpose.

You know you're sitting in your purpose when...

...you feel unsure about your ability to live it.

...you lack confidence in yourself to do what you have been destined to do.

...you feel unwilling to take action and commit to living your purpose.

...you take timid steps instead of boldly going forward.

...you see glimpses of the abundance your gifts can bring into your life and the lives of others, but the glimpses are unsustainable.

You know a company is standing in its purpose when...

...its vision is clear.

...its guiding principles are the foundation of its success.

...teams are collaborating in a positive environment.

...sales are up, and even in an economic downturn, it is agile and it survives.

...it's innovative with a sole purpose that is meeting customers right where they are.

You know a company is sitting in its purpose when...

...profits are down.

...its teams are confused.

...they miss opportunities.

...its employees do not feel supported.

...managers are not effective at organization.

...its operations are not streamlined.

...leadership is not clear.

If you're standing, you can walk, you can run, and you can go forward. If you're sitting, you're going nowhere. You're staying still. If you're sitting in your purpose, you have recognized what your purpose is, but you have yet to take ownership of it, and you have yet to take steps to fulfill it.

Your soul purpose equates to love.

In the last chapter, we talked about the need for self-love and self-acceptance to be able to recognize your true self and your unique gifts. If you're sitting in your purpose, you have recognized your gifts, but you have not yet recognized their value. Your gifts are often the things that seem effortless to you, so it's very easy to take them for granted. This means it's possible to recognize your purpose without recognizing the value of that purpose.

Your circumstances or your bank balance are not a reflection of your value.

With self-love and self-acceptance come an acceptance of your gifts and an acceptance of your purpose. With self-love and self-acceptance, you are able to stand in your purpose. When you stand in your purpose, you commit to live your purpose and you *know* that you will be supported as you do so. When you live your purpose, you will not go hungry. Living your purpose creates abundance, and all that you need will be provided. When you know *what* you are destined to do, and you are *doing* what you are destined to do, you feel a connection to your source of inspiration and a connection to the people you're helping by living your purpose.

Ask how you can best serve your purpose.

When you connect with your inner source of inspiration, you will find the answer to how you can best serve your purpose. Your journey to realizing your purpose will have provided you with ways to connect with others. Your own life experiences can help you help others. If you have experienced limiting beliefs—self-doubt, a sense of not being good enough—or if you have experienced the effects of trying to fit in and trying to conform or always trying to earn love or respect by trying to please others, you already have the tools you need to help others recognize their own value and feel the power of self-love and self-acceptance. If you are living your purpose, you will always be able to serve, and even difficult circumstances can help you serve better.

Nothing you experience in your life, no matter how challenging, is ever in vain.

When you ask how you can best serve and then follow through on the answer you get, you are standing in your purpose. When the answer you get takes you too far out of your comfort zone to go for it, you are sitting in your purpose.

When you sit in your purpose, you severely limit, if not paralyze, your potential to move toward fulfilling it. Imagine yourself in a room with only one door. If you want to leave that room to go somewhere else, you need to go through that door. Sitting in your purpose is like sitting in that room, looking at the door, knowing it's there, knowing there's somewhere else you should be going, but not taking steps to go there. You might approach that door from every angle—walk past it, cartwheel past it, walk on your hands past it— but if you are unwilling or afraid to actually open that door and walk through it, you are unable to leave that room. Leaving that place means opening that door and walking through it, and by the same token, fulfilling your purpose means getting up from where you're sitting and standing in that purpose.

You must take action.

But here's the thing: The action you take must be *purposeful* action. Cartwheeling past the door is taking action, but it's not going to get you where you're meant to be! To be able to stand up, you must question why you are unwilling or afraid to do so. Whatever fears you have, whatever doubts you have, the longer you stay seated, the more power you give them. When you stand up, you empower yourself. When you accept your gifts and your purpose, nothing can stand in your way.

Your soul purpose is what you're destined to do.

Many of my clients over the years have found themselves sitting in their purpose, aware of their soul purpose, yet unwilling or afraid to accept it. In one particular case, my client had recognized her purpose, and she knew how she could best serve that purpose. But *knowing* had not instantly led to *doing*, as it meant taking a giant leap away from her comfort zone. Instead, she continued to work hard at other things, things she felt more comfortable with, but her efforts were not bringing her the outcomes she was striving to achieve. The proverbial door kept slamming in her face because she was not living to her already-recognized soul purpose.

When you stand in your purpose, you recognize that you have nothing to fear because your soul purpose is what you are destined to do. To stand in your purpose, you must not only *recognize* what your purpose and gifts are, you must *accept* them as yours and understand their value. *Your* purpose is *your* destiny, and *your* gifts were given to you so that you could fulfill your purpose. When you stand in your purpose, you have an unshakable faith and belief that everything you need will come to you.

Angels come in different forms.
They will help you live your purpose.

When you accept yourself for who you are and what you're destined to be, you realize that you have everything you need to live your purpose. With self-love and self-acceptance, you no longer need to prove yourself to anyone. You don't need to bend over backwards to please other people, you don't need to give the shirt off your back, and you don't need to keep seeking approval or love because you already have it. When you accept your soul purpose, you realize that you were born with that purpose and the gifts you were born with are the only tools you need to live that purpose.

However, making the move from sitting to standing can feel overwhelming. If you're sitting in your purpose, what is it that's holding you back? What is it that you fear? Be honest with yourself. Are your fears real or imagined? Do you have *reasons* for remaining stuck or stagnant, or are you simply making *excuses*?

Your soul purpose is bigger than you.

If you're feeling overwhelmed, it's time to reconnect with your soul purpose. Refer to the answers you gave to the questions at the end of Chapter One and **be inspired.** Reconnect with your purpose by reconnecting with your source of inspiration. Spend time in an environment that inspires you, and spend time with people who energize and inspire you. Reconnect with the real you and with your soul purpose; then, take a moment to realize that your soul purpose is bigger than you. Whatever your purpose, you don't have to do it all. By living your purpose, you are fulfilling your part, and it's important to realize that beyond that point you have no control, and that's okay.

My purpose is to help individuals and businesses identify their soul purposes and help them monetize them. At one point in my life, I was employed by Microsoft. I was successful in my position, and I enjoyed my job, but I knew that I was not fulfilling my soul purpose in that position. I was not being of the utmost service. I found inspiration in a building that I bought and developed into a day spa for a community that had no similar facilities. I was able to use my gifts and entrepreneurial skills to build a successful business and also fulfill my purpose by providing a valued service for the community at large.

The process of buying a property, applying for loans, and creating a business plan, along with all of the associated paperwork involved in setting up a business was all new to me. I was on a steep learning curve and I didn't have all the answers, but because I was living my purpose, the help and guidance I needed were provided to me.

Not everyone will support you. People will stand in your way. Challenges and challengers will come, but living your purpose means standing in your purpose and standing firm. When you stand firm in your purpose, the people in your life who are not supportive will not stay around. This can feel like a negative experience, but it's really just clearing the way to let better things come into your life. Fill your life with the people and the things that feed your soul.

Accept your purpose.
Stand in your purpose.
Honor your purpose.
Protect your purpose.
Shield your purpose.

Your soul purpose is inspired, so relax. Your unique gifts are yours, and no one can take them from you. Trust in yourself. By honoring yourself, you honor your purpose. The things you need to help you best serve your purpose will come to you, and it's okay to let everything else go. When you recognize your purpose, stand in it. It's *your* soul purpose. When you're standing, it's an undeniable feeling of transformation.

Standing Up

To live your soul purpose, you must stand in it, not sit. Here are the key points to help you stand up:

- Reconnect with your true self and your unique gifts.
- Stay in touch with your soul purpose.
- Accept your soul purpose as your destiny.
- Ask how you can best serve your purpose.
- Have faith and know that everything you need is already yours or will come your way.
- Let unsupportive elements of your life go. They are holding you back.
- Take purposeful action. There is nothing to fear when you're living your soul purpose.

"What we can or cannot do, what we consider possible or impossible, is rarely a function of our true capability. It is more likely a function of our beliefs about who we are."
—Anthony Robbins

CHAPTER THREE
ACCEPT THE ABUNDANCE YOUR SOUL PURPOSE PROVIDES

"Life in abundance comes only through great love."
—Elbert Hubbard

WHEN YOU'RE LIVING YOUR SOUL purpose, great things happen, but some of those happenings may also be losses or what you perceive to be losses at the time. For example, some relationships may not survive, and you may lose a partner or even your job. When you accept the abundance your soul purpose provides, you realize that your loss is, in fact, a loss of something that was familiar to you, rather than a loss of something that was right for you.

If you're not in the right environment for you, you may already know it, but yet you choose not to do anything about it or move on to a new environment because things are okay. You're doing okay with things the way they are. For example, when I was working at Microsoft, I had a good job. I was a manager there, and I approached the position with the view that if I could make it at Microsoft, I could make it anywhere. I had the skills to do the job, but I knew I wasn't fulfilled by it. I was destined to do more, but I was doing well in a big company and earning good money. I wasn't going to move anywhere!

However, living your soul purpose means taking action to stand in your purpose. Before I left Microsoft, I had already put a down-payment on the building in Alabama where I was going to open a day spa. It was my intention to start my own business *and* stay in my job. I didn't have all the answers. I wasn't sure how I'd manage to do both, but I did know that creating a spa for the community was an opportunity to answer my calling, so I went with it. About a month later, I was in Georgia with my family at the time of year when funds are raised to send missionaries on worldwide projects. I gave money to support the cause and effectively gave everything up to God. I left it to Him to let me know if I was doing what was right for me. When I got home that evening, I opened my mail to find confirmation of everything I needed to go ahead with the spa. The following morning, my boss met with me at work, and my relationship with Microsoft was severed. My point is that some relationships can be viewed as a considerable loss at first. I hadn't planned to leave my job, but it worked out that way. When you take steps to live your soul purpose, only the things you need to help you fulfill that purpose will remain in your life. The people or things that fall by the wayside were not meant for you.

When you learn to live your soul purpose, you learn to recognize what's not right for you.

In losing my job, I lost good money, good bonuses, and good everything, but I was called to serve a purpose. I hadn't intended to leave Microsoft and everything it provided, but I was not fulfilling my purpose there. I knew it wasn't my calling, but yet I chose to remain there because things were okay. I enjoyed working with my colleagues. I enjoyed being a part of a winning team and performing well. Losing my job represented a loss of what was familiar, not what was good for me.

My natural gifts had allowed me to acquire the skills that led to a successful career at Microsoft and in a whole range of other industries. Everything I did came easily to me, but I recognized that I had more to offer. I had previously worked in healthcare, and I knew that my work in that area made a difference to people's lives because patient safety was something I felt passionate about. I felt that if I did not perform at my best and implement my gifts in the right way, people would die. I felt that what I did in healthcare impacted lives in a much different and more profound way. At Microsoft I was doing my job and doing it well, but I found that solving problems in different industries was intriguing, although not as fulfilling in the same way that working in the healthcare industry was for me. I stayed with Microsoft because it provided me with a good living, not because it inspired me, and I think many people find themselves in exactly that position.

The fear of losing something is very often the only thing holding you back. When things are going okay, you're afraid to change anything because you're afraid of losing what you have. My message to you is that when you live your soul purpose, abundance will come your way. Whatever it is you need will be provided, and the bottom line is that what you currently have is not necessarily what you really need.

Abundance is your birthright. Your struggle could very well be your transformation.

Creating the spa and providing a service to the people of that community was part of my soul purpose journey. Microsoft fell by the wayside because ultimately, keeping my job there would have prevented me from living that purpose fully. The spa was right for me, and it became a great success. When you live your purpose, you never work again because what you do makes full use of all the natural gifts you have been given. What you do is what you love.

By the age of 31, I was a millionaire. When you're living your purpose, you have to get comfortable with success. Your soul purpose is your destiny, and you have to step into your light. Often people are uncomfortable with success because they are concerned about what other people will think of them. They worry that having more money will cause their friends to view them differently, but really, if your friends are true friends, they'll be happy for you. They may even be inspired by you and want to spend more time with you because you're a positive influence in their life as they look for their own soul purpose. *Expect* good things to come into your life, get ready for them, and make room for them.

There is nothing wrong with abundance.

When you're living your purpose, you are providing a service to the universe. Your ability to make a difference in the world is unlimited, so your ability to attract good things into your life is unlimited. Expect good things. They *will* come. Make room for the abundance that living your purpose will provide by letting go of the things in your life that are not right for you. Focus on what inspires you, and waste no energy running around after things that are not helping you live your purpose fully.

Of course, along with huge ups in life, there can also be huge downs, and I was no exception. The spa business began to struggle, and I faced tough times trying to make ends meet. I went from being of the utmost service in my purpose to potentially not being able to pay the bills, and I eventually sold what was left of the business and became bankrupt. I was at a very low place in my life, but I happened to be in Georgia once again at the time of giving to the missionaries. This time in place of giving money, I gave my time and traveled to Hungary to support the missionaries there who were helping groups of gypsies. My purpose for being there was to provide encouragement to people who really needed it, and this was something my natural gifts allowed me to do.

Accept the abundance that your purpose provides, and get closer to your love.

A company I had been involved with before joining Microsoft heard that I was back in the job market and hired me immediately. I earned more in my new position than I had earned at Microsoft, so my journey had taken me full circle. The loss of my job led to the development of my own successful business, and the loss of that business then led to securing a new job. The events in my life that could have been perceived as losses did not equate to any real sense of loss at all when I realized that my experiences could only strengthen my ability to fulfill my soul purpose and be of greater service to others. Microsoft was a very important part of my journey, and owning my own business was also a very important part of my journey. I was afforded the opportunity to have skills that are successfully honed and transferable to both large corporations and small businesses. Through the challenging times, I have been able to overcome and be transformed, enabling me to relate to business on various levels, both deep and wide. I understand the struggle and the victory, and there is a valuable place for both because without both places, I would not be as successful as I am today. I could not be of the utmost service to the kinds of clients I serve today, both businesses and individuals. The tools that I have developed on my journey and the skills that I have honed along the way have now added to my unique ability to inspire success and achieve results. No journey is in vain. It all serves your purpose.

The bigger the struggle, the grander the transformation.

The more people you can help, the more lasting ripples or waves in the universe you will create.

Something I find very interesting about that point in my life is that when I was at my lowest ebb, a particular song was placed in my heart, and the lyrics kept repeating in my mind. In my conversations with God, I was told that one day I'd be singing that song for others, and singing it internationally, but at that time, I was struggling through my own challenges. In all honesty, I felt like I just wanted to be locked in a cupboard and left alone to sing my song! However, during the time I spent in Hungary, I *did* sing my song for others many times—up on a stage at a gypsy fair on one occasion—and it was a way of sharing something that had encouraged me with others who also needed encouragement.

The song is titled "I Am Blessed" and sung by Rachel Lampa.

I Am Blessed
I may never climb a mountain so I can see the world from there
I may never ride the waves and taste the salty ocean air
Or build a bridge that would last a hundred years
But no matter where the road leads, one thing is always clear
I am blessed
I am blessed
From when I rise up in the morning till I lay my head to rest
And I feel you near me, you soothe me when I'm weary
Oh Lord, for all the worst and all the best
I am blessed
All along the road I've traveled, I have crawled and I have run
I've wandered in the winds and rain until I've found the sun

But watching eyes have asked me why I walk this narrow way
There may never be a reason for the hope I have today
You give me joy, you give me love
You give me strength when I want to give up
You came from heaven, I gave you my soul
You are the reason that I know, I know
I am blessed...

After singing the song for others in Hungary, I then also sang it for my grandfather at his 80th birthday celebration in Jamaica. What I had been told would happen *did* happen, even though it wasn't something I had put anything into. It confirmed for me that the message was divine and that everything I was experiencing on my journey was part of what was already destined for me.

At the time of losing everything, I learned things I'd never even had to consider before. I learned how to stretch a very limited budget by setting up payment plans for utility bills and everyday essentials. I faced new challenges with each new day, but every time I faced those challenges, they were taken care of. I was broke, but I realized I could hand over control to God. By learning to lean on Him as my Father, I was able to accept the abundance that living my soul purpose provided. When you live your purpose, you will not go without. My personal experiences taught me that even when your circumstances appear outwardly to be less than ideal, if you're walking your soul purpose, everything you need will be provided, and your perceived losses are, in fact, gains that will help you to better serve your purpose.

When you stay focused,
abundance will come your way.

Challenging circumstances can make you uncomfortable, but when you focus your energy into the things that keep you closer to your love, the things that don't support that love will disappear from your life. The loss of certain things or certain people may cause you to shed a tear, but it can be helpful to think of it as shedding your skin: What you lose is only lost to make way for something better.

> *"What the caterpillar calls the end of the world,*
> *the master calls a butterfly."*
> —Richard Bach

Your soul purpose comes from a place of love, and when people or things are not right for you, their presence in your life can prevent you from experiencing the power of that real love. For example, a couple may choose to stay together even though the relationship is no longer good for one or both of them. One partner may constantly make excuses for the other's disrespectful attitude towards each other, or the partners may only be sticking together because they have children. However, when you find your soul purpose and begin to live it, you learn to recognize the things in your life that do not represent real love. In relationships, just like in jobs, we sometimes hold on to things because they're familiar, not because they're right for us. When you're living your purpose, "putting up" with things is no longer acceptable.

It's not always going to be easy to let go of familiar things in your life, even when you recognize they are not right for you, but living your purpose means making space in your life for the things that *are* right. Living your purpose means accepting the abundance your purpose will provide. Make room for the good things that are coming your way, and don't be afraid to let go of the things that are no longer helping you.

*"Everything you need, you already have. You are
complete right now. You are a whole, total person, not
an apprentice person on the way to someplace else. Your
completeness must be understood by you and experienced
in your thoughts as your own personal reality."*
—Wayne Dyer

Some physical things that happen to you can be perceived as losses—losing a partner, a job, a house—but when you're living your purpose, these things are not to your demise. These things are only clearing the way to allow room for better things to come your way. When you're facing challenges, it can be difficult to stand in your purpose and to let go of the things that are not supporting you in that purpose, but if you stand firm, better things are waiting for you just around the corner—a wonderful partner, a more fulfilling job, or a bigger house.

A great example is American businessman Lee Iacocca. His relationship with Ford Motor Company broke down, but an even better relationship was then able to begin with Chrysler Corporation. Iacocca actually entered the motor industry as an engineer, but he very quickly recognized he was not fulfilling his purpose and moved into sales. His rise through the ranks to become the president of the Ford Motor Company illustrates beautifully that when you're living your purpose, you will be successful. Iacocca's natural gifts catapulted Ford to record sales and profits, but he was then fired from the company because of on-going clashes with Henry Ford II. Losing his job could have been viewed as a significant loss, but he was snapped up instantly by Chrysler. At the time, Chrysler was on the brink of collapse, losing millions of dollars, and Ford, by comparison, had just posted profits of over two billion dollars. Once again, his new position could have been viewed by some as a step backward. However, Iacocca reversed the fortunes of the Chrysler

Corporation by using his gifts of innovation and developing the very ideas he'd been blocked from pursuing through disagreements at Ford. The loss of Iacocca's prestigious position at Ford was clearly not to his demise, and by living his soul purpose, he was able to move on and enhance the lives of a great many people. Iacocca embraced his soul purpose as his destiny, and he accepted the abundance that living his purpose would provide. Joining a company on the verge of bankruptcy held no fear, as he knew he was walking his soul purpose and that whatever he needed would be provided.

> *"The thing that lies at the foundation of positive change, the way I see it, is service to a fellow human being."*
> —Lee Iacocca

When things end, whether it's a job, a relationship, or anything else, it's time to move on. Losses can be discouraging, but your soul purpose provides love, and the benefits of that love are:

- Increased health
- Increased finances

Love elevates you. It makes you lighter.

When you accept the abundance of that love, you receive:

- Joy
- Lightness
- Peace
- Understanding
- Knowing
- A positive guiding presence

When I was told to bring joy to people's souls, it meant bringing them love—real love. A very powerful example of real love can be found in my sister's story. My sister and her husband lost their first child exactly six months to the day after his birth. The death of a child is not a loss that anyone is going to be able to move on from easily, but they found their way together. Their philosophy is that if God had come to them before the arrival of their baby and asked them to accept the gift of their child, to take care of him, love him unconditionally, and then give him back to Him after six months, they would have wholeheartedly accepted the gift. That's love.

My sister's words at my nephew's funeral…

…I spoke to my mother soon after Baby Isaac's death, and she said,"I hope and pray that God is finished recruiting angels from my family." I told her it was better than someone else recruiting from her family.

I was touched by the resolve of my mother-in-law, Daisy Mae Starks from Natchez, MS, who told me, "Girl, don't question God, 'specially when he just calling back what came from him."

I thought on that, and my mind went back to a day a few short weeks ago, almost three to be exact, when I sat here in the front row with my husband, my child, and family and friends, and dedicated my baby back to God.

It was, hands down, one of the happiest days of my life.

And when Pastor Chappell spoke of the significance of Isaac in the Bible and how God spoke and asked Abraham to sacrifice his firstborn son and how Abraham complied, I thought about what faith that must have taken. I quietly asked myself if I would have been willing to give my child to God in faith...and I reluctantly thought, "yes"... not knowing, of course, that God would so soon call myself and my husband on that commitment.

A test of faith. A difficult test.

And after a life spent believing that God knows what is best; and that life's situations ought to be left in God's hands; and times spent in prayer reiterating that His will be done, I knew in my heart that His will would not always align with what I hoped and prayed, and that the same way we accepted the vast array of blessings that He has showered down upon us through the years, we had to accept this: the loss of the physical presence of our one and only son.

Are we alright? It's a question that keeps coming from all of our concerned friends and family. The honest answer is that we are greatly saddened and profoundly shaken by the passing of a baby that at home we referred to as "Peanut" — what he looked like when we saw the ultrasound for the first time and when he was born—"Little Man"—because he got so big so fast;—"Big Man"—because he kept growing and somehow "Little Man" seemed inappropriate;—"Honey"— I'm not sure why. I just couldn't stop calling him that.

Our hearts are broken, but we are supported by our faith. A faith that creates perspective in the midst of sorrow. God has given us a glimpse into HIS perspective and has made it ours.

He knows that if He had taken us aside as a couple and said, "Here's the deal, I've got this baby, a perfect happy angel sent by Me whom I am entrusting to your care for six months, at the end of which I am calling him home…"

We would have said yes and would have gladly accepted the honored position of being God's specially chosen foster parents.

God knows that.

Are we alright? Our lives have been touched by God in the form of a little boy that brought us more joy in six months than some give in a lifetime, and when God puts that kind of joy in you and plants it firmly at the roots, you can't help but come back to that. When you've been touched by God, sorrow can only visit where peace and happiness permanently reside.

Our only child is gone and we cannot change that, but we're not crazy for feeling blessed even now. We have support. How many others have gone through these challenges alone? Look at the sheer number of people in this place. Tell me that is not a blessing. Our child was not sick for one day of his life; he did not suffer in death. We were able to provide for him.

We miss little Isaac deeply, yet we are at peace with his passing. If someone had told me my baby boy would pass away two weeks after his christening, I would have told them I couldn't possibly bear it … I would have thought I would be looking for somebody's bridge to jump off of. I always wondered what peace that passes all understanding was … until now.

We mourn, but we cannot stay down for long because God delivered what He promised and what we prayed for, a healthy, happy, alert, smiling baby, who underwent no strife or struggle, even unto his death a moment that came about quietly, just after he finished playing with his favorite toy.

Baby Isaac had a perfect life, full of love. What more could any parent want for a child? We have been comforted by your love and support during this difficult time and if attendance today is any indication, it seems our little boy has touched a greater number of lives than we could have ever anticipated. We are grateful for the honor and privilege of being his earthly parents. We pray that God would shower down blessings upon your lives as He has ours.

God Bless our child. God's child. Isaac DeWayne Kelly Jr.

My sister accepted the abundance of love her soul purpose provided, and she now has two children, two beautiful, healthy boys.

Accepting Your Abundance

- Accept that when you are living your purpose, abundance will come.
- Accept that abundance will be yours, and begin to prepare for its arrival now.
- Accept that preparing for the arrival of your abundance means clearing the way and making space.
- Accept that the loss of people or things from your life is only a loss of the familiar, not a loss of things that were good for you.
- Have faith, believe, and know that everything you need will be provided and that the people and things that are right for

you, or even better for you, are waiting for you just around the corner.

Sabine's Story:
Soul Purpose Branding

"I believe we all yearn to be seen for who we are,
not what we do."
—Sabine Messner

I dreamed of being an artist and of living a big life.

I'm originally from Germany, but I've been living in the United States since the mid-'90s when I came here in pursuit of a spiritual calling.

The first inkling I had of my life's vision was around the age of six. I grew up in a small village in the Black Forest where life was rural, simple, and backwards. Therefore, I always looked forward to seeing Hollywood movies on TV, and I especially loved all the singing and dancing of the musicals. I was thoroughly convinced that this is how life should be. It was then that I decided to become a famous actress or an artist—someone who goes out into the world and actually lives the sort of life that others just watch on screen. My parents gave me permission to take over the entire attic, where I literally furnished an imaginary world that I would slip into on a daily basis after school and homework were done. We had lots of vintage clothes from at least three generations and various eras, which gave me plenty of ways to act out my fantasy plays. My envisioned world became so real that when I think back to my childhood today, I have vivid memories—if not sometimes even heightened memories—of my enacted daydreams, which are sometimes even brighter than factual reality. It was that little girl who, at an early age, had made up her mind and began living her dream in an attic full of possibilities.

My dad taught me the technology of transformation.

My father was an inventor, an alchemist, and a visionary—a true trailblazer in his own right. Growing up I spent a lot of time helping him in his laboratory, where he invented hydrogen car engines in the early '70s, high-pressure water pumps, and all sorts of other amazing patented creations. He was especially fascinated with perpetual motion, centrifugal force, and water-oil based emulsion— all principles that he turned into highly advanced prototype engines. Entering my dad's laboratory was like crossing over into a different dimension, an inner world full of ideas, emotions, and experiments. Between learning about the elements as well as basic mechanics, my dad taught me how to go straight from a vision in your mind's eye, to a quick sketch on a piece of paper with lots of black fingerprints, to a real functioning engine that would run flawlessly for decades and decades. He was never one who did a lot of technical drawings. When it came to his inventions, there was no back and forth since he never doubted his Divine downloads, and for that matter, neither did anyone else. The blueprints in his head were so clear and precise that he could always implement them right away and then perfect the machine iterations as he went along. My father's brilliance lit a spark within me, too. I always felt special being around my big creator-daddy. Every day with him was an adventure, a pursuit of a bigger goal, a better future, a well-oiled engine. Yet, we never arrived. We never reached a finish line.

When I was 17 years old, my father passed away as the result of a brain tumor. It was a tragic event, and I did not want to let him go. I was by his side when I saw his soul leave his body. It was at that point that I realized I could see beyond ordinary reality. A fraction of my soul went with him into the Upper World. I could see another dimension, a heavenly place. I knew I was left with no choice. I was going to have to fully realize my own dream because my father's dream had been so tragically aborted before he could reach a sense of completion. My father's passing made me angry about dying in vain. Since I didn't want to die with any of my potential unfulfilled, I went for my dream with a trailblazing ferocity. His death gave me the jet fuel I needed to take off.

I felt jet-propelled toward realizing my dream.

One year later, I finished my schooling and moved to Berlin, which was a big transition. I was accepted into one of the best art universities in Germany—a great privilege because at the time they only allowed about 30 people into their annual program out of more than one thousand applicants. I studied feverishly and soaked up everything—painting, sketching, black and white photography, all the classic arts—you name it, I did it! Ultimately, I graduated summa cum laude in both my master's and bachelor's degree in Visual Communication. My education encompassed everything from traditional art, such as portraits, nude chalk sketches, abstract painting, mixed media, comic illustration, silkscreen printing, etching, welding, and all the way through computer animation and graphics. In 1993, I created a virtual Internet art installation called "Fishing for the Heavenly Body" for my master's work. The piece was way ahead of its time and anticipated the collective, collaborative, human interaction of the World Wide Web. It was through this innovative and visionary art installation that I was able to land a dream job at *Wired* magazine a year later and become one of the first web designers in the world.

I gave my dream a chance because of a spiritual calling.

As a young girl, I dreamed of Hollywood, but in my 20s I wasn't exactly attracted to America in the same way, perhaps because of the Cold War and the fact that I lived in Berlin, which at the time was still a divided city. It was a fluke that I ended up going on an art trip to Manhattan in October 1991 with my Polish graphic design professor. However, the moment I landed in The Big Apple, I felt like I was coming home, which was a total surprise to me. I'd traveled extensively and been to Africa and lots of beautiful cities all over Europe, but I'd never experienced this intense sense of belonging anywhere else. I felt immediately compelled to separate myself from my student friends because when you're in a group, you can't listen to your inner voice so clearly. I really felt I needed to walk around the city on my own. One evening I was sitting by myself on a bench in Washington Square Park when I had a glorious epiphany.

As I sat on the bench, I saw the early-evening skyline lit up behind the historic park as I watched two policemen majestically riding by on horseback. I must have spontaneously tapped into the—I guess what you could call—quintessential collective "American Dream," one of the most exciting dimensions of human potential. I could literally *see* thousands of souls arriving from the old countries and landing in great anticipation on Ellis Island. I could feel the hopes and prayers of these ambitious, courageous people, each in their own way eagerly wanting to shed their past in the pursuit of their new future. As they reached for their highest goals, they erected skyscraper after skyscraper until the city itself became a living statement of human ambition in all of its glory and brutality.

I had completely merged with the promise, power, and beauty of this place, when all of a sudden a bright shaft of light came down upon me, and I heard a deep voice in my head saying very clearly, *"Sabine, if you want to live your highest purpose, you must move to the United States."*

I was astonished and could only say, *"What?!"* Then the voice continued to say, *"And you will find your highest soul mate."* That was the end of the transmission, and the light shaft disappeared. There was no explanation as to how or why this occurred, yet I knew that everything was going to be different.

In that moment, I was altered. I had tapped into human potential.

I was both excited and mortified by this experience. I was planning on getting married to a beautiful Berliner, my first love. The thought alone of moving to another continent felt like a shock. After I returned to Berlin, my relationship fell apart within mere weeks. I tried to explain to my fiancé that I simply needed space to understand what's happening to me as a consequence of this light shaft experience. He simply couldn't grasp why, from one day to another, I had left him emotionally. We had been together for almost seven years. I loved this man deeply, yet I tragically broke his heart into a million pieces, only to follow some unnamable force that was driving me into a mysterious direction I couldn't even explain. It was a real low point in my life, and I lost many more friends because I became strangely obsessed with my bizarre need to go to America. I couldn't articulate my reasons; I could only offer comparisons in an attempt to justify my terrifying decision. I managed to completely polarize my life to the point where I had effectively stripped myself of everything I had come to rely on, except my determination to bring out the best in me. For me to be faced with the choice of my highest purpose wasn't a question of love, it became a question of life or death.

I could no longer keep my old life together.

After my spiritual calling broke up my relationship, I devoted myself solely to my studies for the next few years. Where I was an art student before, I became a scholar of the arts, through and through. I couldn't just walk through a museum anymore. In looking at a great piece of art or listening to a great piece of music, I literally *experienced* the artist and the process of making art, eventually becoming the piece of art itself. My multi-dimensional ability to connect, not only with the creative process and its final product, but with the person's essence who was the source of it all, was unlike anything I had known before. During these years, I can honestly say that the muses were with me as a new artist was born.

One month after I graduated with an M.A., I was on a plane to San Francisco. A few months later, I was offered the position at *Wired* magazine, which sponsored my work visa. I had the great privilege to apprentice directly with Barbara Kuhr, one of the four co-founders of *Wired*, and later continue to work side by side with her as we designed the World Wide Web's inaugural online magazine.

The Creator is not cruel. I firmly believe that whatever purpose is put into our hearts, we are also given all the tools we need to fulfill that purpose. For me it was never a struggle to have success. Everything I'd ever gone for and put my best foot forward toward, I achieved and succeeded in. I've never been let down by my dream. The struggle was accepting it and surrendering to it. Whenever I've allowed myself to be taken over by purpose, I was always, always taken care of.

The struggle is accepting that purpose and surrendering to it. It's a difficult switch to flip.

Success is going to fall into your lap because it's meant to, but only after you accept your purpose and remain devoted to it. Once you've turned that switch, you must continue to surrender to your purpose on a daily basis. That's the key, and that's where most people give up because it's a serious challenge at the beginning. Don't get me wrong. Even though my personal life is like proof in the pudding, it's still not an easy thing for me to do, even today. Why? Because you give up control and put your purpose in charge, day after day.

After several years at *Wired*, I was at the peak of my career, having become somewhat of a hot commodity in the late '90s, but frankly, I was burned out and had lost my passion to live a fast-paced top designer life. Being an obedient, soul purpose student, I quit *Wired*, got married, and went off on a spiritual journey. I spent time studying with Native Americans, apprenticed with a Tibetan Lama, and essentially went on a spiritual training and discovery journey that led me to study with the Qero Incas in the Andes to learn more about the soul purpose that brought me to the U.S. in the first place. My job at *Wired* was the umbilical cord to my new life, but I didn't come here to just have a successful career.

The soul journey may gift you with a career, and it may also take you out of one. You may not know where it's going to take you next. It's like a two-way street. For all your efforts, you are being most generously rewarded. For all the things that come effortlessly to you—money, opportunity, friends, gratification, fulfillment, and satisfaction—ultimately you have to trade back in some of what you've worked so hard to create in order to open up space again for new growth. Acknowledge the beautiful things you've been given, and then let them go, as you would shed a skin in order to grow into a fresh, new, even more beautiful one.

Today I can see the big picture, and it's a beautiful one.

Today, I humbly look at my life from a high plateau where I can finally see how all of its puzzle pieces fit together in such a magnificent way that I would have never been able to plot. The things I perceived to be losses have turned into treasures. Detours have revealed themselves as destinations. Wounds have turned into faith, discipline into beauty, art into life. Everything has unraveled itself as having been absolutely necessary and absolutely good—the breakdowns, the breakthroughs, the break-frees—including the various dark nights of the soul—yes, I've had a few of them too. What matters is that I'm now embarking on my ultimate purpose, and that is to help as many souls as I can possibly touch to leap into their highest destiny and create the lives of their dreams through self-propelled, heart-centered entrepreneurship. There's nothing in this world that gives me more joy than to be of service in exactly this way.

Once people connect with their potential, there is no such thing as a small soul purpose. It doesn't exist.

It's all about making it possible for people to step into their own purpose and start monetizing it by making it a reality. There's a huge need in the world for people to activate their soul purpose because when they do, they too can offer the world the biggest transformation in their own unique way. One person's soul coming on fire lights the way for hundreds and thousands of others to follow. This is how we each propel one another forward. Collectively speaking, there's a great sense of urgency around each and every one of *us* doing this work *now*, not tomorrow, not the day after tomorrow—but *right now*.

There are many ways in our existence that we cannot sustain any longer, including the way we exploit our resources and the way we operate on greed. It's *us* living our purpose and *us* finding a new way to exchange gifts and services that makes us the bridge builders to the new economy and the inhabitants of a New World, such as the one we've always envisioned as children in our heart of hearts.

Our planet is going through a massive death and rebirth process as we speak. Faced with unfathomable earth challenges, each and every one of us stepping into his or her highest purpose is the most hopeful, rewarding, and magnificent way for us to create the future we actually want to experience. As the Hopis predicted, *"We Are the Ones We've Been Waiting For."* You and me, we are alive right now to fulfill this promise. So what's it going to look like? How do we do it?

I see people as the highest representation of themselves.

We start with the ultimate end in mind—our most cherished dreams. My gift is that I witness people in their highest potential and then translate that potential through transformative art into a personal Soul Brand that positions them on the web—for life. My process is a one-stop destination, linking spirituality with strategy, with artistry, and finally, technology. I have method, education, training, and experience to achieve all of this in one intense transformation. I guess you could say I do hands-on healing with people's futures so that it's no longer a silent dream, a repressed longing, a bitter, sarcastic outlook. Together with an eager and capable client, we turn possibility into probability, and eventually, reality, through the conscious alignment of purpose, design, and technology. Often people may have a spiritual awakening but don't know how to express their realizations. What can take someone years to figure out, we can do in months. And that's a good thing because we're out of time.

I feel that I don't have to do any explaining anymore. I can just be. It's like I can let go, and my own life container, my business, is holding me.

Although I'm still in the foundation phase of building my own business, I've recently made a final and deliberate leap, and that is the decision that I'm not employable anymore. There's no longer an employment environment that allows me to fully live my purpose. I've outgrown all of them. Instead, I now use all of my gifts and all of the skills I've learned, and I'm turning them into the foundation of my enterprise. My talents, in effect, have become my own economy; my spirituality and creativity are now my new currency. To me there is no better job security than to be doing what my soul came here to do. You jump out of bed in the morning with excitement, and it's the easiest and most natural thing because it's you. It's just you. There's no outside performance stress, just an invitation to be your best and a calling to do your best. You walk out into the world, and you don't have to prove or justify anything anymore. You are simply a living expression of your purpose. You're doing what you've been divinely designed to pursue.

I've finally freed myself from the need for approval.

I confess that I used to have a strong need for validation and approval. It's the most ironic thing since I'm such an independent person. Most people would never think that I'm a recovering approval-addict since I don't usually come across that way. Where did this need for approval come from? Perhaps, it's something that may have stemmed from my cultural upbringing, perhaps it has to do with my cross-cultural identity, or perhaps it's a personality thing, or an astrology thing, or a numerology thing or a mixture of all of the above. Honestly, I don't have a clue. But what I do know is if I were to pinpoint the single, biggest hindrance I've encountered in my life—especially around living my soul purpose—it's my former addiction to approval. This is, again, the most ironic and ridiculous observation, since no one else can approve your soul purpose but you!

The need for approval clouds your clarity, compromises your confidence, and weakens your courage—all crucial qualities you need to pursue your purpose. Thankfully, approval has never stopped me, but it definitely did slow me down. If I didn't care as much about other people's good opinions, I would have let go sooner, surrendered much earlier, and simply done it bigger, louder, and bolder. I would have known that by just listening to my inner voice and stepping into my light, so much approval, admiration, and validation would have come my way anyway. I now feel I want to be an exhibitionist in my soul purpose. Let everyone see me naked. I've set myself free. I am who I am.

Sabine Messner
Founder, PowerReinvention
www.powerreinvention.com

CHAPTER FOUR
BE UNAPOLOGETIC

"In our home there was always prayer—
aloud, proud, and unapologetic."
—Lyndon B. Johnson

TO BE SUCCESSFUL, YOU MUST have confidence. It takes confidence to stand in your purpose, but when you've found inspiration and you're making your own fingerprint, you must have confidence in yourself and what you're doing.

If you can't believe it, you can't expect others to believe it.

Don't hide from your gifts, and don't undersell yourself just to accommodate other people around you. Be unapologetic; be strong in your belief that you're doing what you're destined to be doing in your soul purpose.

Speak with authority. When you are living your soul purpose, you have self-acceptance and love, and you have influence. Tap into those things, show your passion, and step into your light.

A client of mine had a background in wellness and fitness. She was very successful in her career and everything she did came easily to her, but because of that, she felt she wanted to branch into something more challenging. Her belief was that if something was harder, it would be worth more. It was also her belief that staying in her current career would not earn her the income she wanted because lots of others were already providing the same service. In fact, she was already sitting on a gold mine, but she didn't recognize its credibility because it came easily. Her motivation to change direction and create a new enterprise was high, but progress was slow and success was not coming easily. This led her to realize that her soul purpose was to be of service in her original wellness-oriented career. The transformation in her as she "found her mojo" and really began to feel her soul purpose provided a great example of being unapologetic. When she was not living her purpose, she was a quiet, unassuming, squeaky presence in a room, but when she accepted her gifts and returned to living her soul purpose, she transformed into a shining light in a room, exuding energy and passion in everything she was saying or doing. She was now speaking with authority because she knew she was doing what she was destined to do. She knows it, she feels it, and she's passionate about it, so she's no longer timid.

When you recognize your soul purpose, be authoritative and show your passion by not being timid. Know that no one else can offer exactly what you offer, and no one else can do what you do. There may be many others with similar titles, but there's only one you. Your gifts are unique to you, and no one can do what you do better than you. Be unapologetic about your uniqueness.

When you finally have it, when you really know what you're on this earth to do and who you're supposed to serve, you know exactly what gift it is that you have to offer. You are destined to provide a service to people, or to your tribe, even though you're going to face opposition. Your tribe is the group of people you are here to serve. You can call it a community or your clients, but the point of a tribe is that you're here to serve them with your gifts. Your tribe is determined by the fact that you have gifts they need, and by making yourself available to them, they can find you.

It's important to understand that you don't have to cower away from what you know you are here to do. Whatever you discover your purpose to be, not everyone is going to see it that way. When you are able to clearly identify what your uniqueness is, it's going to be something that no one else has. You will have a unique way of slicing what your offering is, and it might not be something that is commonplace; it might not be something that allows people to put you in a perfect little box. Don't be discouraged by people not being able to neatly categorize you; don't look for that kind of approval. Be unapologetic about who you are and what you are offering, and stand firm in your soul purpose.

Georgina's Story:
NUMBERS
WITH PURPOSE

"I finally feel like I fit my skin."
—Georgina Terry

I'm originally from London in the UK, but I have now lived in Trinidad for 10 years. I started my career as an accountant, then moved into the area of change management before discovering that what I have a gift for actually had a name, and that's coaching. I never quite fit into the typical accounting box, but I loved being an accountant because of my affinity for numbers. It represented a necessary stepping-stone toward finding my real niche and my soul purpose.

One of the greatest inspirations in my life was the book *The Seven Spiritual Laws of Success* by Deepak Chopra. Through that book, I came to realize that even though you might see your gifts as just something you naturally have, you still feel compelled to improve on them if you wish to serve others. When I read that, it moved me to tears because I realized that what I'd been doing naturally even before I knew I was doing it (coaching) *was* something I wanted to be able to do to the best of my ability. The book was talking about me. I wanted to be able to give more and be of even greater service, and it was at that point I knew that this was what I was born to do.

I thought my gift was just something everybody had.

Throughout life, I was always told that I had really good interpersonal skills, and I knew that I could connect well with people. However, because it was something that came naturally, it wasn't anything I always took much notice of. Even in my teens, others were recognizing my relating skills, but because it was so natural, I really didn't see it as a big deal. In fact, I thought it was just something that everybody had. It was only when I started working in my 20s and met people who did not have "any" interpersonal skills that I realized that I had been blessed with some GREAT powers.

My parents brought us (my siblings and me) up to believe that we could be anything we wanted to be in life as long as we wanted it enough. If we could see it, taste it, smell it, or touch it, we could achieve it. I grew up thinking that *everybody* had the same belief and knew they could be and have whatever they wanted.

I wanted to be able to give more and to be of even greater service, and it was at that point that I knew that this was what I was born to do.

At the age of 16, I'd decided that I was going to become an accountant. Not *wished* I would be an accountant, but *DECIDED* I would be one and *KNEW* I would be! I chose this profession because it is not industry specific. It's totally flexible because accountants are needed no matter what the economic climate looks like. It was also a profession that presented the opportunity to work for yourself or work for a company, and at the time of making the decision, there weren't many women in the finance industry. That, in itself, was a pull for me!

People automatically assume that if you're an accountant, you must be a mathematician, but I'm really not. I just have a good understanding of numbers, and am not afraid of them. I see myself as an interpreter of numbers. I can understand numbers because I see beyond the actual numbers to see what they are telling me.

My first job was with the *Economist* Newspaper (commonly known as *Economist* Magazine), and I started taking my accounting exams while working there. Even then, whenever I met someone and explained that I was an accountant, they'd always say, "You don't strike me as an accountant." I didn't fit the "normal" profile, and I always described myself as being unique. I then moved to a prestigious firm, Coopers and Lybrand (now PricewaterhouseCoopers), and was promoted several times before eventually becoming financial controller.

During my time at PwC, while managing a team of eventually 22 people, I started to formally help others achieve their goals. My focus was very much on developing my team, and I did begin to notice the power of my interpersonal skills.

It was only then that I realized that maybe what I had wasn't something everyone else had.

Something very interesting about my initial interview to join the firm is that after I was put forward by the recruitment agency for the role, I realized that I was capable of doing more than the job required. However, I decided to use the interview as practice, rather than cancel it. During the interview, the finance director realized that I had greater skills than the role needed and commented that I could do more than the job offered, so he took out a blank sheet of paper and, between us, we created a new role, MY new role! You don't have to squeeze into an existing box to fit in. You just have to be yourself.

> *"Whatever the mind of man can conceive and believe,*
> *he will achieve."*
> —Napoleon Hill

When I realized that not everyone saw or knew that they could achieve anything they wanted, it was the beginning of my understanding that I had a gift to see beyond what was right in front of me. Due to my parents' influences and teachings, I can see beyond where I am. I can see and feel where I want to go, but the *how* is not important. If the vision is clear, the *how* will fall into place. This gift of "seeing" beyond allows me to help others achieve the same understanding and sight in their own lives and businesses. My work as a coach is my way of helping others to see that they have that gift too, which enables them to live their lives by desire and design, rather than by default.

Over time I became curious about what people wanted to do with their lives and what their goals were. I really wanted to help people move forward and achieve their goals in life.

By working alongside consultants when I was at the peak of my accounting career, I became interested in what they did and wanted to know more. I knew a lot about finance and thought if I could learn what they knew about business, I would increase my marketability! I saw a job vacancy that appealed to me and applied for it, even though I knew I didn't have all of the specified requirements. I went for the interview and got the position. They had chosen to interview me on the strength of my previous experience, and they then hired me because of my personality. They saw me as someone who had the right personality, and they knew that the other skills were things they could teach me.

It means I'm able to say to people that if they really want something, they should go after it. You need to put yourself in the ring; you never know what will happen. It also highlights, once again, the importance of just being yourself. I didn't have all of the skills listed on the job description; I didn't fit neatly into the specified box, but it didn't mean I couldn't fit in. By just being myself and not pretending to be anything other than myself, I was recognized as someone who fit in for simply being who I really was for communicating what I had to offer.

I felt like I was home.

The company's business model was very much centered on linking business with people. It was about developing people to deliver results, so I felt like I was at home. I'd found my niche. It married my two worlds of understanding how to increase the bottom line and my understanding of developing people by empowering them to achieve their maximum potential. Joining this new company enabled me to realize this thing, this gift that I'd always had, was actually called something, and that something was coaching.

A year before finding my niche as a coach, I'd written down some goals for myself. Those goals were to change jobs in order to move into consulting, to buy a property, and to work in Trinidad because I'd always wanted to work abroad. As I was writing the list, I was trying to figure out which order I should put them in, but I realized that the order was unimportant. I just needed to set out some goals. One year later, I found the list and saw that all of the goals had been achieved, even though I hadn't consciously carried the list in my mind. The consulting job I now had, gave me the opportunity to work and to move to Trinidad within weeks of accepting the position, and not only that, it gave me the opportunity to realize another goal—riding in a helicopter—as I worked off-shore for over a year on an oil rig!

Everything shifted and fell into place.

As a child, I'd dreamed of collecting stamps in my passport, and I've traveled so much now that they keep filling my passports. Before I moved to Trinidad, I was someone who liked certainty in life, and perhaps that's why I was attracted to finance and the certainty of numbers. I liked things to be structured, right or wrong, and in effect, I'd been brought up to see life in that very black or white, right or wrong sort of way. The move to Trinidad opened up the opportunity to see life differently, as it represented a shift away from certainty. It was a time of transition as I moved into a new work environment and to a place where I didn't know very many people and no longer had the certainty of everything being familiar around me. It was a tough transition, but I came through it. I remember writing down one day, "I no longer see only black and white; I see beautiful color."

Reaching the point where I was able to see beautiful colors meant I was able to see so many more perspectives. I recognized that things didn't always have to be right or wrong, and several things could be right or several things could be wrong. There didn't always have to be just one answer. It allowed me to embrace life and, in effect, come back into my gift, as I was able to see different perspectives without holding anyone in judgment. When clients are talking to me, it makes no difference where they're coming from because it's my goal to help them get from wherever they are to wherever they want to be. It's not about where I am or where I want to be. It's all about them.

I embraced life by embracing my gift.

Part of my coaching process is to ask clients to visualize themselves in the future. I ask them to create a mental picture of themselves achieving what they're truly capable of. It's an incredibly powerful exercise. So often people have never allowed themselves time to think about what it is they really want to achieve in life, and it's only once they have that opportunity that they come to realize what it is they *really* want to do and be. Once they have that vision, they can then think about how they're going to get there. What's interesting is that when I started to think of having my own business, for the first time in my life, I didn't take the time to fully visualize what that actually meant for me. I had to work through the process of dealing with doubts and questioning whether it was something I could do. I just knew it was the right thing and the right time, even though I didn't have a clear vision, which was very unusual for me.

Taking the first step toward starting my own business was a huge leap of faith. I was moving from the security of a six-figure salary into what was basically the unknown. A year before taking that step, I'd set myself the target of saving up a year's salary to establish a cushion, but I hadn't set any clear targets of what I'd aim to achieve once I'd taken that step. It took me a long time to transition my mindset from employee to entrepreneur. I recognized that I had what I needed in terms of helping others to achieve their goals and maximize their potential, but I needed additional skills to be able to grow my business, which I didn't understand. I hadn't fully understood that I needed to know about sales and marketing and the power of networking because previously, as an employee, my mantra was that my work speaks for itself, so I don't need to shout about it. But now I *did* have to shout about it. As an employee, you walk into the structure, but as an entrepreneur, you have to *create* that structure.

I'm now able to just be.

Now, as the "Passion to Profitability Expert," I'm able to just be. There's no box to fit into as there was in accounting or in consulting. There's no "norm" to fit into. However, I realize that all of the positions I've held previously are all part of who I am and what makes me, me. I no longer cling to certainty, and I'm comfortable to just let things evolve by doing what comes naturally to me. When you are able to fully accept yourself and just be yourself, opportunities will come to you, and you will create them too, effortlessly. When you accept your soul purpose, what you need comes to you; it comes naturally because you are in service. When you are in complete service, the universe will serve you. When you accept the assignment that God gave you, you will be provided for. It's only when you're able to truly accept yourself and your gifts that you're able to live your purpose fully.

Accepting yourself and your soul purpose allows you to trust in yourself. By trusting myself, I've been able to step out of my comfort zone and do much more than I anticipated, for example, writing my own book, *The Amazing Race to Entrepreneurial Freedom*, which became a bestseller. Through that, I've been able to create a ripple effect that extends far beyond Trinidad and the people I physically come into contact with. I've also been able to lead the way in co-creating the first ever female entrepreneur workshop "IGNITE," which is held in Trinidad, and I've been asked to be a keynote speaker in the U.S., which actually challenged me to trust even more in myself because the topics stretched me beyond my normal presentation subjects. As a result of just being me, a great many doors of opportunity have opened for me, and great things have and are happening. Things that I didn't go after have found me. When you're able to love yourself, you're able to fully *be* yourself. Loving yourself is all about trusting yourself and trusting in yourself to be you. I finally feel like I fit my skin. I love being Georgina Terry and all that she is and will be.

Georgina Terry FCCA
The Passions To Profitability Expert
Director, Business and People Development Associates Limited
www.bpdassociates.com

CHAPTER FIVE
BE YOUR OWN
FINGERPRINT

"Wherever you go, go with all your heart."
—Confucius

WE ARE ALL UNIQUE. WE all have our own unique fingerprint to impress on the world. When you're living your soul purpose, you have confidence in the fact that there is no one else in the world who can do a better job of being you than you. You also know that fulfilling your purpose means just being you and not an imitation of someone else.

Your fingerprint is unique to you. Fingerprinting is a recognized method of identifying individuals, along with eye scanning or voice recognition security systems. Your fingerprint represents *only* you. Of course there are other people in the world who may appear outwardly similar to you, or they may be doing similar things in life to you, but they are not you. It can be discouraging to see other people achieving things you've yet to achieve, especially when they appear to share similar gifts to you, but that's when you must remember that only *you* can be you. Everyone has their own unique gifts. You don't need to achieve what others have achieved; you don't need to be like anyone else or do better than anyone else. You only need to be the best that *you* can be in whatever it is that *you* do.

Only you can be the best at being you.

You bring your own unique offerings to any situation. People may share your hair color or your skin color. They may have the same qualifications that you have or do a similar job, but the difference is that you have your own unique soul purpose. Only *you* can fulfill *your* soul purpose. You have been put on this earth to provide a unique service to the world, and no one else can provide that service.

If you're living your soul purpose, everything you need is at your fingertips. When you're walking in your purpose, you're providing a unique service to the universe, and your uniqueness will attract others into your life. The right people will appear at the right time. You already have everything you need to fulfill your purpose. The people who are drawn to you are drawn to your uniqueness, not necessarily your ability to fit neatly into any of life's boxes.

Your uniqueness is what makes you, you. Your unique gifts have been given to you to allow you to live your soul purpose and be of the utmost service to the universe. For example, a group of gifted musicians may form a band. They are all living their soul purpose by being a part of that band, but they all have their own unique offering to give. One band member fulfills his purpose on drums, another on guitar, and another as lead vocalist. We all have souls, but we also all have our own unique soul purpose. The stage is large enough for everyone. There's room for everyone to shine.

When you're living your purpose, you're not going to be doing exactly what the person to the right or left of you is doing because your offering to the universe is uniquely yours. When you're being of the utmost service through your soul purpose, no one can provide *that* service better than you. Using the band example again, when each individual in the band steps forward to the front of the stage, a different group of individuals in the crowd will cheer for each one. The members of the crowd are drawn to particular members of the band because of their uniqueness—a unique energy they give out, perhaps.

We can come together as one, but our unique fingerprint will always identify us.

Never be discouraged by others doing what you do. There are other bands, other drummers, other vocalists, but there's no other you. We all have our own soul purpose to fulfill and our own unique gifts to allow us to fulfill it. You are the only, and the best, version of you.

Your fingerprint represents:

F	freedom
I	intuition
N	never giving up
G	growth, greatness
E	evolution
R	reciprocity
P	prosperity
R	respect
I	influence
N	natural
T	time

Freedom

When you are living your soul purpose, you are free to be who you are, and you are free to let everything else go; you're free to let go of the things that are holding you back from being yourself and fulfilling your soul purpose. Being your own fingerprint is an uplifting experience because you recognize not only who you are, but who you are not, and you are free to just be.

Intuition

When you are living your soul purpose, you will receive guidance along the way. Intuition is a very powerful internal guide, but not everyone listens to or gives credit to the little voice they hear inside their mind. When you are being your own fingerprint, you have the confidence to follow that little voice.

Never Giving Up

Living your purpose doesn't guarantee that you won't come up against challenges or barriers, but when you are able to be your own fingerprint, you realize that the barriers are only perceived barriers and the way around them will come to you. When you're being your own fingerprint, there is never any reason to give up.

Growth

As you live your soul purpose, you will grow. Your confidence will grow, your abundance will grow, and the quality of your relationships, both personal and professional, will grow.

Evolution

The more you live your soul purpose, the more you evolve in terms of finding ways to be of the utmost service in your purpose. You evolve by identifying more opportunities to be of service and to make the best use of your gifts.

Reciprocity

As you live your purpose, you are able to give to others by being of service, but you are also able to receive by attracting good things into your life. In return for the flow of energy you give out to the people who are attracted to you, you receive a continuing flow of energy through them. When you accept your soul purpose and recognize your fingerprint, you open yourself to receiving the people and the things that will help you to fulfill that purpose.

Prosperity

When you are living your soul purpose, you will prosper. Expect to prosper. When you are your own fingerprint, the people and the things you need will come to you. When you are being of the utmost service in your soul purpose, the people you serve also prosper.

Respect

Your soul purpose is a gift. Respect your gift and respect yourself. When you accept yourself as your natural self and you accept your uniqueness, you gain the respect of others.

Influence

When you live your soul purpose, it has a ripple effect. When you recognize your fingerprint and step out confidently as yourself, your gifts will influence others. If you're a songwriter, your lyrics will influence all who hear them. If you're an athlete, your athletic ability will influence and inspire others.

Natural

Your soul purpose is natural. When you're living your soul purpose, everything has a natural flow. Your natural gifts are often the things you do effortlessly, so when it feels like you're swimming against the tide, you're working against your soul purpose.

Time

The time is now. When you recognize your soul purpose, you don't know how much time you have to live that purpose, so waste no time chasing the things that are not meant for you.

You're designed in a certain way, a way that allows you to live your purpose. It doesn't matter how society views you or what your outward appearance is; it's who you are and what you do when you're living your purpose that creates your fingerprint. It's not your look that defines you. Outward appearances can change; a person may have an accident and lose their sight or a limb but their soul, their destiny, and their unique fingerprint remain unchanged.

Even in groups within society, members of the group have their own personality and their own uniqueness to offer the group as a whole. Your design gets tweaked along the way in response to your personal experiences in life, allowing you to grow and become more and more fulfilled as you become better equipped to be of the utmost service through your soul purpose. You might be a lawyer in a firm of lawyers, but the way you deliver your message will be different from the delivery of the others, even when it's the same message that's being delivered. You might be a dancer in a troupe of dancers, but the way you respond and move to the music is going to be different from how the others do, even when dancing to the same music. Two singers can sing the same song, but each rendition is uniquely different. Your fingerprint is always uniquely yours in whatever it is you do, and no one is going to be better at being you than you.

> *"At bottom every man knows well enough that*
> *he is a unique being, only once on this earth;*
> *and by no extraordinary chance will such a*
> *marvelously picturesque piece of diversity in unity*
> *as he is, ever be put together a second time."*
> —Friedrich Nietzsche

My own evolution, in terms of recognizing my fingerprint, came through the dating process. I already knew my soul purpose; I had recognized and accepted my unique gifts, so I knew that all I had to do when I was meeting new people was just be me. People were either going to like me as me or not, but I wasn't worried about it because I already had self-acceptance and love. I was my own fingerprint, so all I had to do was be myself. I was not in competition with anyone else, and I didn't have to pretend to be anyone other than myself. The people I met may have wanted to meet someone who was quieter than me, louder than me, younger or older or different in some other way, but I didn't feel pressured by it because I was my own fingerprint. Being your own fingerprint brings with it a sense of peace, an acceptance of who you are in all your uniqueness.

There's a comfort in knowing and accepting who you are and also in knowing that your own precious fingerprint is all you need to be accepted in this world. At the time of being invited to interview for a position at Microsoft, I was not someone who knew a whole lot about the computer industry. I felt very privileged to have been invited, so I felt I should take a trip to my local Barnes & Noble bookstore and browse through some books on the subject beforehand. When I walked into that store and discovered that the computer section was not the shelf or two of related titles I had imagined, but aisle upon aisle of books on computer technology, I once again realized that the best way to approach the interview was to just be myself: to be my own fingerprint. I wasn't going to be able to absorb all of the information in those books anyway, so the best thing I could do was put my best self forward, which meant just being me. By the end of the interview, I was offered a position, and that offer came my way because I was my own fingerprint.

My unique gifts were recognized by Microsoft as something that could move the company forward. I was able to use my existing knowledge of technology and my skills as a change agent to approach companies in a way that focused on *them* and helped them identify *their* needs and then, almost as a by-the-way, introduce them to the Microsoft software that could meet those needs. If I had approached my interview with Microsoft pretending to be something I wasn't—someone with a finger on the pulse of the latest Microsoft technology—I would have completely missed the mark in terms of what the company was looking for. My soul purpose is to help others fulfill their own soul purposes. At Microsoft I was able to help companies identify their sole purposes and achieve their business goals, and in the process, help Microsoft fulfill its purpose.

I think many people miss the mark in terms of realizing that all they need to do to be successful in life is to be their own fingerprint. When you're living your purpose, you will be successful in whatever it is you're doing to fulfill that purpose. If you're chasing things in life that are not right for you, things that are not helping you live your soul purpose, you will not find the success you're looking for. If you're comparing yourself to others all the time and competing with others in everything you do, you're effectively trying to be someone else's fingerprint. Everyone's fingerprint is unique only to them. Success doesn't come from trying to be someone else. Success comes from being yourself and being your best self by being your own fingerprint.

> *"He who trims himself to suit everyone*
> *will soon whittle himself away."*
> —Raymond Hull

There was a time when being a model meant being a certain height and weight and being a blonde with blue eyes. If you wanted to be a model, that was the "norm," and that was how you had to look, so aspiring models went to extremes to achieve it. Of course, things then changed, and a new body shape was needed, a different weight, or a different length of hair, so the "norm" became something different. Extreme measures were needed once more to be able to achieve the latest look. If you're going against the grain of your natural self and trying to be something or someone you're not, you're not being your own fingerprint. It's not about trying to be a certain type of person or trying to be just like someone you admire or even trying to be better than someone. It's about being yourself and accepting yourself for who you are naturally. Your gifts are the things that come naturally to you. Different things come naturally to different people. Everyone has their own soul purpose and their own unique fingerprint.

You only need to be yourself to be your own fingerprint.

The USP (unique selling proposition) of a company is what makes that company uniquely different to all the other companies listed under the same heading in the classifieds. By recognizing its uniqueness, the company will be of the utmost service to the clients who value its USP, and it will be successful. If the same company tried to be all things to all people, it may well fail to attract the same level of success. The success of a company is dependent on its ability to recognize, value, and promote its uniqueness.

The closer you get to your soul purpose, the more you learn to recognize your uniqueness and learn to articulate it to the world. The more people you can reach, the greater your ability to be of service to them. By accepting and promoting your uniqueness, you attract into your life the people who can benefit most from what you have to offer and also the people who can help you fulfill your purpose.

When you represent your fingerprint, you know that you don't need to be all things to all people to be successful. When you're dating, you only need to be yourself. The people who want you to be something else are not right for you. When you're going to a job interview, you only need to be yourself. If you don't get the job, it wasn't the right job for you. When you're in business, you need only find and promote your USP to find your success. By being your own fingerprint, you accept the abundance that will come your way, and you are able to accept that you don't need to be anything other than your true self to be successful in fulfilling your soul purpose.

When you understand what your unique fingerprint is, it becomes your responsibility to let other people know about it. The more you accept your soul purpose, the more you stand in your purpose, the greater your ability to reach the people you are destined to serve in that purpose. The more transparent you are about what your fingerprint is, the more you will attract the right people for you or your business.

When you're not living your soul purpose, you won't know what your fingerprint looks like. If you're sitting in your purpose, opportunities will pass you by. When you accept your purpose and stand in it, you learn to recognize your fingerprint. When you know what that fingerprint looks like, you gain a clear understanding of who you're destined to serve through your soul purpose. It's not possible to be all things to all people, and by recognizing your fingerprint, you also learn to recognize who you need to reach in order to best serve your purpose.

By being your own fingerprint, you are no longer in competition with anyone else. You recognize that you only have to be yourself to find success. For example, if you are designed to be a sprinter, your gifts will be cultivated by training specifically as a sprinter. Attempting to train as a long distance runner at the same time will be counter-productive to your success. It's not possible to train effectively in both disciplines, and it's not necessary to do both in order to be successful. Being your own fingerprint makes it possible to recognize who and where you have been designed to serve your soul purpose. When you live your purpose, success will be yours.

"Learn to ... be what you are, and learn to resign
with a good grace all that you are not."
—Henri Frederic Amiel

Gary's Story:
A HEALER
WITH PURPOSE

"To be a servant doesn't mean you need to be a slave. Servants get paid; slaves don't."
—Gary Barker

As a rule, I don't often talk about myself, but sometimes people come along who perhaps need a little bit of inspiration in life, and I'll tell them that I was 40 years old before I went to chiropractic school. This is my way of letting them know that it's never too late to do something you want to do in life.

My passion is to help people.

I have a passion for helping and serving people, and I think that's a key factor in my life. I'm a chiropractor, but I'm a chiropractor because I have a passion and the compassion to help others through the natural healthcare system. It's through chiropractic science that I'm able to do that by freeing up the interference with the nervous system and then supporting that with nutritional advice and other technologies.

I'm originally from Pennsylvania and I'm the oldest male child in the family. I have two older sisters, a younger sister, and a younger brother. I have only four cousins, so we're a small clan. We grew up in a fairly rural town, but it was also fairly wealthy due to the oil and lumber industries. My father worked in the dry-cleaning industry with my grandfather, but he had issues with his lower back and suffered headaches as a consequence. He would often visit an osteopath, and I'd go with him. I was around 12 years old, but Dr. Gahring showed me how to work on my dad, and through the course of time, I practiced working on him and other members of the family. I then became an Eagle Scout, and a big part of scouting is to be of service to others. In fact, the Boy Scouts have two mottos: "Be prepared" and "Do a good turn daily," which I believe helped to cultivate the person I am today.

Every day I ask myself: what good turn have I done today?

When I graduated from high school, I thought about becoming an osteopath, so I asked Dr. Gahring about it. He told me that I would have to look at becoming a chiropractor because in the 1960s, osteopathy lost its identity to the medical profession, moving toward prescription drugs and away from manipulation therapies. At the age of 18 when my parents were going through a divorce, I mentioned my thoughts on becoming a chiropractor to my mother, but her response was not favorable, so I thought it was not the right thing for me to do. However, I did continue to practice working on people, and they continued to get better.

My father then took a new job in Tulsa, and I moved there and became very ill at that time with tonsillitis. As a family, we didn't take many drugs, preferring a more natural approach, but I was treated with penicillin, and within a couple of hours my body reacted. I had spots on my abdomen, and then my body began to swell. I itched from the top of my head to the soles of my feet, and I actually passed out and went into a coma.

When I woke up three days later, I weighed about 10 or 15 pounds less, and I was extremely weak. It took me six months before I could stay awake for eight hours. I didn't take another prescription drug until I was in my 50s and had to have a hernia repaired. I do not believe in taking drugs except under extreme circumstances, so I have a very biased slant against medicine. In my own experience, using drugs did not have a great outcome, consequently, I work within a natural healing profession. In chiropractic, we know that nerves control and regulate all functions in the body, so if you can remove the interference from the nervous system, the body can heal itself as it's intended to by our Creator. We're designed to be self-healing and self-regulating, and as long as we don't have interference, we can do that. My job as a chiropractic healer is to help people understand where that interference comes from and help them eliminate that interference so that they can heal.

Only you heal yourself; nobody can heal you but you.

In my grandfather's dry-cleaning company, we did just about everything ourselves, so I grew up doing things with electricity that only licensed electricians would do today. I was exposed to steam lines, air lines, and water lines and had experience working with all those different things because it simply wasn't affordable to bring people in from the bigger cities. When I was still at school, my first job was a bookkeeper for a local plumber, but when he realized who my grandfather was and found out what I could do, I began to work in the plumbing industry. Through that I became a maintenance manager for an apartment complex, then got into the construction industry where I framed houses and, over time, worked in the restaurant industry, bought and sold jewelry, and worked as a private investigator. Somewhere along the way I got married.

I worked in many industries but never lost my passion to help people.

The passion to help people never left me. It was always there, and I'd find I could help people by doing what Dr. Gahring had taught me. I'd manipulate their spine, they'd get better, and on we'd go, but it seemed to me that every time that happened, something would occur in the businesses I was in and sometimes it would be quite profound. One time I had a partner in a remodeling business, and most of our clients were in the banking and oil industries. In the early '80s when those industries hit hard times, most of our clients disappeared, but I'd been treating a young woman who suffered migraines. Even though we'd lost business clients, I found I had a waiting list of private clients who wanted work done on their homes.

Every time I helped someone, good things happened.

My marriage didn't work out and I thought again about going to chiropractic school at that time, but I didn't like the school in the area where I lived. I moved to Florida, remarried, and became a punch-out man, which meant I would go to properties to fix and straighten out any problems left behind in the construction process. One day I tripped over a hose in a garage and hurt my back. I knew I needed to go to a chiropractor, and it didn't even cross my mind to go to an M.D. While I was being treated, I mentioned that I'd thought of becoming a chiropractor myself, and he said, "What's stopping you?" It struck me at the time that I didn't have an answer.

Everything was okay, so I stayed where I was.

I had what I considered to be a good job, I made a decent living doing what I did as I'd progressed in the construction industry, and I had designed and built my own home for my family. Everything was okay, so I suppose I had just stayed with what I had. But, the housing market then dipped, and the company I worked for as a construction manager had to let me go.

Ironically, I ended up working as a cabinet maker in the very houses I'd previously managed. Providence is an amazing thing; I was in a job that I knew wasn't going to last long, and I wasn't making the money I previously had, but it did essentially free me up to consider other things. On my last day, I was in my truck when it was hit by a gentleman backing out of a driveway. He was really concerned over whether I was hurt, and he let me know that if there was anything he could do for me, I was to let him know. I told him I needed a job! It turned out that his job was hiring employees for Disney, and a few days later, he called me to offer me a position. It wasn't a very taxing job compared to what I was used to doing, but it did afford me the opportunity to continue going to school to get the prerequisites I needed so that I could attend chiropractic college.

My second wife had surgery on her jaw that involved the use of a Teflon material, and at that time, the material was recalled—can you imagine having your face recalled! It caused her a lot of pain, both physically and emotionally, and resulted in us being unable to see eye-to-eye. I saw a counselor during that period who surprisingly had a very similar background in life to my own, almost a life parallel to mine, and he said something to me that he'd never said before as a counselor—"You need to get divorced." I knew then that

I had to make changes in my life, and I was inspired by something I heard a motivational speaker say: "People don't like to change, but everybody likes to improve." I made the decision to go to chiropractic college, and from that point on, everything began to fall into place.

I had to make changes.
I had to move from where I was.

Before starting my studies, I went to spend some time with my mother. It was during that time that I met the woman who is now my wife. She was with me through all of my studies and is very involved in the culture of natural healing, so it's a match that works really well.

When I started college, I literally had my truck, my tools, and a thousand bucks in my pocket. I found a place to stay that cost $200 a month, and I was asked to give a down payment of $100 at the college. I had no idea where I was going to get more money from, but I knew it would be provided. Close to the college, I found a subdivision and presented myself there as "the best punch-out guy around *and* available to work evenings and weekends." They hired me on the spot! I actually worked 25 - 30 hours a week and went to school with a class load of 25 hours a week, but I still managed to graduate. When I did, I was $104,000 in debt and had no assets other than my truck and my tools.

Through traveling around the country to visit my brother and sisters, I saw several places where I could consider setting up a business. I'd settled on an area that best suited me, but I needed to borrow money to set myself up in business. Being new to business and having no assets, I was fortunate to find a banker who understood my circumstances and helped me through the process of organizing a loan. In 1998, I opened my chiropractic office. I had a good relationship with my banker, so I chose to continue dealing with him even when his bank moved him to a different location. One day I discovered he was no longer there, and his secretary called me to say there was some paperwork connected to my loan that I needed to sign. When I looked at the papers, I realized that it wasn't accurate. She just looked at me, rolled her eyes and said, "Oh please, just sign the papers."

The business did really well. I paid back the loans in no time and then found a property to buy and convert into my business location.

When you're living your purpose, the people and the things you need will be provided.

Later in life I came across an old journal I'd kept back in 1978. In it I'd written that I would become a chiropractor, and I'd signed it with my name, followed by the initials D.C. (Doctor of Chiropractic). It was 1998 before I opened my office, but it highlights how important it is to set goals and to create a vision in life because I believe writing that goal down subconsciously set in motion the process of getting to where I am today. I really believe I was chosen to do what I do, and I believe everyone is chosen to have a great impact in life, if they listen.

Our job as human beings is to constantly improve ourselves.

When I was in school the first time around, my focus was more on my out of school activities than on my grades, but when I returned to school, it was because I wanted to get the grades so that I could get where I wanted to go—chiropractic college. When you have a goal, you have a focus.

Providence is a wonderful thing. I was meant to be a chiropractor; I was meant to be a healer. I was 40 years old before I started my training in college, but here I am. I'm aligned with my purpose, and everything is in place. I work with an enormous range of cases, but I do seem to attract fairly unique cases.

One gentleman had seen three or four chiropractors before me *and* had two surgeries, but I know that I can help anyone who shows up, no matter what their history, given the appropriate amount of time. This gentleman had excruciating back pain, and he was worried that he was going to have to get out of the business that had been in his family for generations. He thought he would have to give up work and start taking disability payments. As it turned out, I was able to help him, and he's now working and is now able to do virtually whatever he wants. I do still see him though, and I've been doing so for ten years.

A young lady came in because she wasn't getting pregnant, and now there's a child out there because of that. A five-year-old boy had been diagnosed with "failure to thrive" and had a number of complications since birth that involved surgery and a variety of medical treatments. He told me his feet hurt just standing up, his lips were blue, and he never moved during his examination or treatment, which was very rare for a child. He was unable to blow up a balloon because of his herniated diaphragm, but within weeks, he proudly stood in front of me and did just that. That's a really profound example of healing. When you remove the source of the interference, the body is able to heal itself.

Another lady was 85 years old when she came in, and she had excruciating back pain. After her first treatment, she went home and was able to reach up to take a cup out of her cupboard, something she hadn't been able to do for almost 20 years. It took just one adjustment to improve her quality of life.

A gentleman who had seen a lot of doctors came in one day. As I examined him, I asked if he'd lost a lot of weight recently, and he told me he had lost around 40 pounds in just a couple of months. A sudden weight loss like that is a red flag for cancer, and although as a chiropractor I can't diagnose cancer, I was able to x-ray him and tell him something was not right with his bones. I had to refer him to an oncology doctor, but I also continued to treat him. He kept coming for adjustments because it made him feel better, never great, but better, and he had someone bring him to the office two days before he passed away because the adjustment still made him feel better. It gave him a higher quality of life, even though he knew he was dying. That's the difference that chiropractic makes; that's what I do. It's a great reward to be able to do that, a reward far beyond the monetary gain.

I believe you have to follow your heart and follow your passion.

I can look back and question how things might have been if I'd pursued a career as a chiropractor when I was 18 years old instead of when I was 40 years old, but I know I've learned a great deal about people in the interim. I'm able to communicate very well with everybody because of the life experiences I've had. I can communicate equally well with a corporate manager or a construction worker because I can relate to them. It's my life experience that gives me my unique fingerprint as a chiropractor. Maybe I wasn't ready at 18, or maybe I just wasn't listening. The path that worked for me is not necessarily the path that's right for someone else, and we all have to follow our own path. My self-esteem changed over those 20 or so years, and I believe if we could teach young people to improve their self-esteem, they'd be in a better position to listen when the passion strikes and that little voice inside tells them, "This is what you need to do; this is where your gifts are; this is how you will help humanity."

I really believe that our main function in life is to serve humanity, but to be a servant doesn't mean you have to be a slave. Slaves don't get paid, servants do.

So many people are slaves to their jobs, and they hate what they do. Consequently they *are* a slave, and they don't get rewarded for what they do. People need to understand who they are, so they can understand what they love. When they have a passion for something, and they love what they do, many times the rewards will be there, and that's the key. Find your passion.

Gary T. Barker, D.C.
Doctor of Chiropractic
Portland Chiropractic
www.DrGaryBarker.com

CHAPTER SIX
GIVE BACK

*"If you have zest and enthusiasm, you attract zest
and enthusiasm. Life does give back in kind."*
—Norman Vincent Peale

WHEN YOU'RE LIVING YOUR SOUL purpose, a flow of energy is created, and giving back is an important part of maintaining that flow. You might give back by donating money or volunteering your time to causes you feel passionate about, but by giving back, you keep that energy flowing. Giving back is a way of solidifying the abundance that's coming your way. When you're living your soul purpose, the people and things you need to help you fulfill that purpose will be provided for you. By giving back, in whatever form that takes, you're giving back to the universe.

Everyone experiences ups and downs in life, and there can be times when you feel that the demands being placed on you, in terms of finances or time, are so great that giving back becomes difficult. However, continuing to give back in whatever way you can is what keeps the circle of energy flowing. As you give, the energy you give is returned to you, and what you need will come.

Your soul purpose is all about love. When you give back, you complete a circle of love.

Giving back enriches your life in many ways, and it's often when you're giving back that you experience a great many unexpected benefits. When you're living your soul purpose, you're sharing your gift and your energy with the people you are here to serve, and you receive energy from them in return. Giving back to the universe in any small way can make an enormous difference to the lives of other people, and completing that circle of love is an uplifting experience that energizes everyone involved. It's often when you feel you have nothing to give but you give anyway that you receive the greatest love in return.

> *"Thousands of candles can be lighted from a single candle, and the life of the candle will not be shortened. Happiness never decreases by being shared."*
> —Buddha

Giving back ensures that the flow of energy doesn't stop when it reaches you. When you're living your purpose and doing what you love, you will feel so full of energy that giving back comes naturally, but there may also be times when you're feeling like you're at a low ebb and your natural tendency is to hide away from others rather than actively look for ways to be of service. It's during those times that giving back is of even greater benefit. If you hide away to dwell on your own troubles, the flow of energy stops with you. If you take the focus away from yourself and focus on doing something for someone else, the flow of energy is maintained. If you hide away, you isolate yourself from the universe, but by giving back, you stay connected to the universe and what you give will come back to you in the form of what you need. It's not all about charity or giving to causes that other people feel you should be concerned about. It's about giving back to the things in life that inspire you and that you feel passionate about.

Giving back re-energizes you.

When you're living your soul purpose, you accept the abundance that it provides. When you're able to give financially, you're able to understand that there's always more of what you have coming your way, so it's not necessary to hold on to every penny. Holding on to what you have would only stop the flow of energy.

The Wise Woman's Stone

A wise woman who was traveling in the mountains found a precious stone in a stream. The next day she met another traveler who was hungry, and the wise woman opened her bag to share her food. The hungry traveler saw the precious stone and asked the woman to give it to him.

She did so without hesitation.

The traveler left, rejoicing in his good fortune. He knew the stone was worth enough to give him security for a lifetime. But a few days later, he came back to return the stone to the wise woman.

"I've been thinking," he said. "I know how valuable the stone is, but I give it back in the hope that you can give me something even more precious. Give me what you have within you that enabled you to give me that stone."

—Author Unknown (courtesy of InspirationPeak.com)

Edwene Gaines is a leading prosperity teacher who overcame poverty to live a lifestyle of wealth. In her book *The Four Spiritual Laws of Prosperity* she demonstrates that the solution to financial problems lies within and explains why it's essential to tithe to the person or place where you have received your spiritual nourishment and to follow your divine purpose in order to live a life of true prosperity.

> *"Prosperity is the manipulation of spiritual substance and bringing it into form as matter so that we can use it in the physical world."*
> —Edwene Gaines

Giving back becomes something you do automatically. It's not something you do egotistically; it's not something you think long and hard about. It's a natural response to the abundance that comes your way. The people and the places you automatically give back to are those that have inspired you in some way on your journey. For example, at one point in my life I felt inspired to donate to a college fund. When I was in college, I knew a number of students who were only able to attend because they received financial assistance with their tuition fees. Getting a college education is something I feel passionate about, and at the time of donating, times were getting harder for students and their families. I gave back by donating to a fund that would provide others with the opportunity to attend college.

If you need more money to help you fulfill your soul purpose, I strongly recommend that you give back by donating money to causes that inspire you. When you receive money by being of service through your purpose, give back a percentage of that money to a cause you feel passionate about. Edwene Gaines encourages everyone to give back 10 percent of what they receive, but I know many people who automatically give back much more. By giving back financially, you are accepting the financial abundance that your soul purpose provides. It's also important that you give money on a regular basis and continue to do so. Financial giving is not something you should do only when your finances have received an added boost. It must simply be something you do. It's not the actual amount you give that counts; it's the commitment to continue giving back a dedicated percentage that matters.

Develop a habit of giving back financially and then look for ways to give more by giving your time. This is particularly important if you're financially wealthy because giving your time provides an opportunity to give more of yourself. For people with low incomes, a willingness to give back financially maintains the flow of energy. However, for those with high incomes, financial giving can almost go unnoticed, so giving time as well as money can be a powerful way of enriching and energizing their own lives and the lives of others.

Opportunities to give come into your life in the same way that the things you need come into your life. Giving back maintains your connection with the universe and your soul purpose and maintains the flow of energy. The people and places that provide inspiration for you in your soul purpose will also inspire you to give back. Stay connected to the things you feel passionate about, whether they are environmental issues, homelessness, or animal welfare, and opportunities to give back will present themselves. It's not as cut-and-dry as a 10 percent debit on your bank statement; it's about love.

When you're living your purpose, your intention must be to maintain the abundance that serving in your purpose provides. Giving back maintains the flow of energy that brings that abundance your way. To continue moving forward in your purpose and to keep making a difference in the world, you must maintain that flow of energy. Maintaining that flow means continuously giving back, not just occasionally giving back. Keeping up the momentum in the way you give back will keep up the momentum in the way you receive what you need to be of service through your soul purpose.

Everything in the universe is comprised of energy, and our thoughts, feelings, words, and actions all form part of that energy. Energy moves in a circle—what goes around comes around—so everything we think, feel, say, and do comes back around to us to create our realities. There are a number of Universal Laws that help us understand how cause and effect are related and demonstrate how certain patterns of behavior will enhance our physical, emotional, and spiritual growth.

There are 12 Universal Laws in total, with the following being of particular importance in relation to giving back:

The Law of Divine Oneness
We are all connected. Everything we think, say, or do affects others and the universe around us.

The Law of Action
Action must be applied to manifest all things on earth, so our thoughts, dreams, emotions, and words must be supported with actions.

The Law of Cause and Effect
Nothing happens by chance or outside the Universal Laws. Every action has a reaction or a consequence; in other words, "we reap what we sow."

The Law of Compensation
This is the Law of Cause and Effect applied to the blessings and abundance that are provided for us. The effects of our deeds become visible as gifts, blessings, money, inheritances, and friendships.

By not giving, you're only hurting yourself. When you don't give, you miss out on great opportunities to grow. When you don't give, you weaken your connection to the universe. When you're not giving, you potentially sabotage yourself emotionally, spiritually, and financially. Giving is not just about the receiver. It's every bit as much, if not more, about the giver. When you give, you strengthen your giving muscle, and as you continue to give, that giving muscle grows stronger and stronger. The stronger you become as a giver, the stronger your impact becomes, the greater your influence becomes, and the wider your reach becomes. Not giving weakens your ability to fulfill your soul purpose and make a difference by being of the utmost service through your purpose.

Not giving can have catastrophic consequences. A powerful example of the effects of taking without giving back can be found in the story of Easter Island, a remote island in the Pacific Ocean. Now uninhabited, there was once a population of around 7000 Polynesian settlers. There are many myths surrounding the demise of the Easter Island inhabitants, but one of the most compelling theories is that a developing attitude of "bigger is better" ultimately became their downfall. As the initial handful of settlers multiplied into larger extended family groups, social organization began to develop. Closely related households formed into clans, and each clan was headed by a chief. It was this organization that led to rivalry among the clans and ultimately, the collapse of society on Easter Island. Each clan had its own ceremonial site, which was used for burials, ancestor worship, and the commemoration of past clan chiefs. The chief monuments were large stone platforms, but with the cultivation of crops for food taking relatively little time, increasing elaborate monuments began to appear. The "bigger is better" and "more must be better" culture grew through competition between the clan chiefs, and the giant stone statues synonymous with Easter Island today were the result. Historians believe the statues must have been moved from the inland quarries to the coast on tracks made of rolling logs. Trees would have been cut down in ever-increasing numbers, and it was this deforestation of the island that had catastrophic effects on the inhabitants. They depended on wood for housing, fires, canoe building, and making fishing nets. The removal of trees also caused the island's soil to become eroded, so crop yields began to decline, as did the population. The people of Easter Island brought about their own demise by taking from the environment in ever-increasing quantities and giving nothing back in return.

People who continually take without giving back will never be fulfilled in life. Whatever they have will never be enough, and they will always want more.

The Stone Cutter

There was once a stone cutter who was dissatisfied with himself and his position in life. One day he passed a wealthy merchant's house. Through the open gateway, he saw many fine possessions and important visitors. "How powerful that merchant must be!" thought the stone cutter.

He became very envious and wished that he could be like the merchant. To his great surprise, he suddenly became the merchant, enjoying more luxuries and power than he had ever imagined, but envied and detested by those less wealthy than himself. Soon, a high official passed by, carried in a sedan chair, accompanied by attendants and escorted by soldiers beating gongs. Everyone, no matter how wealthy, had to bow low before the procession. "How powerful that official is!" he thought. "I wish I could be a high official."

Then, he became the high official, carried everywhere in his embroidered sedan chair, feared and hated by the people all around. It was a hot summer day, so the official felt very uncomfortable in the sticky sedan chair. He looked up. The sun shone proudly in the sky, unaffected by his presence.

"How powerful the sun is!" he thought.
"I wish I could be the sun."

Then he became the sun, shining fiercely down on everyone,
scorching the fields, cursed by the farmers and laborers. But a
huge black cloud moved between him and the earth so that his
light could no longer shine on everything below. "How powerful
that storm cloud is!" he thought. "I wish I could be a cloud."

Then he became the cloud, flooding the fields and villages,
shouted at by everyone. But soon he found that he was being
pushed away by some great force, and he realized that it was
the wind. "How powerful it is!" he thought. "I wish I could be
the wind."

Then he became the wind, blowing tiles off the roofs of houses,
uprooting trees, feared and hated by all below him. But after
a while, he ran up against something that would not move, no
matter how forcefully he blew up against it—a huge towering
rock. "How powerful that rock is!" he thought. "I wish I could
be a rock."

Then he became the rock, more powerful than anything else on
earth. But as he stood there, he heard the sound of a hammer
pounding a chisel into the hard surface, and he felt himself
being changed. "What could be more powerful than I, the
rock?" he thought.

He looked down and saw far below him the
figure of a stone cutter.

—Buddhist Parable

The most common reason for not giving is a fear of being left with nothing. People believe they can't afford to give, but the truth is they can't afford *not* to give. By not giving, they isolate themselves from the universe, and the flow of energy stops with them. Abundance can only be theirs by giving back to the universe and maintaining the flow of energy. Giving can never result in being left with nothing, but not giving can. Sometimes people keep hold of what they have because they believe it's the only way to keep themselves ahead of the rest. If you really want to stay ahead, you have to give back because the only way to get hold of the things you need to get ahead and then stay ahead is to maintain the flow of energy between you and the universe. Give to the universe, and the universe will give to you.

There can also be times when people are discouraged from giving because they feel they have so little to give. It's their belief that what they have to give is so insignificant that it's not worth giving. This is where gaining an understanding of the Universal Laws connected to giving can be life-changing. It's not the amount that counts; it's the giving. Being willing to give back to the universe in whatever small way you can results in the universe providing all you need in return.

Everyone has something to give. My grandmother was someone who always gave whatever she had to give whenever anyone came over to her house. This might have been nothing more than something to drink and whatever food she had in her kitchen, but by always giving, she always had something to give.

> *"There is nothing insignificant in the world.*
> *It all depends on the point of view."*
> —Johann Wolfgang Van Goethe

By committing to give back 10 percent of what you receive, the 10 percent of someone's $50 earnings per week is every bit as powerful as someone else's 10 percent of their $5,000 earnings per week. However, it's important that giving back is not about percentages and calculated returns; it's about staying connected to the universe and your soul purpose. Giving back is about maintaining the flow of positive energy; it's not about profit margins.

If you place no limits on what you can give, you place no limits on what you can receive.

Giving Back

- Commit to giving back on a regular basis.

- Give back to the people and things that inspire you.

- Give back to maintain your connection with the universe. The universe will provide the abundance you need, so you can never earmark what you give back with a specific return in mind.

- Give to strengthen your giving muscle, and never be discouraged if the receiver does not use what you give in the way you intended. Go on giving.

CHAPTER SEVEN
BROADEN YOUR HORIZONS

"If you do not feel yourself growing in your work and your life broadening and deepening, if your task is not a perpetual tonic to you, you have not found your place."
—Orison Swett Marden

EVERYBODY HAS A SOUL; IT'S a common denominator. As long as you're living and breathing, you have a soul. When you live your purpose, you begin to connect with people on that soul level, and there's no limitation. When you're able to communicate your purpose, you're able to connect with the people you are destined to serve through your soul purpose, and you begin to create a ripple effect that reaches far beyond where you physically are.

For example, the gift of music can reach a global audience and transcend every culture. A song can be popular around the world without the need to understand the language of the lyrics because the rhythm and energy of the music are enough to connect with the souls of listeners everywhere. When I was in Hungary with the missionaries, I noticed that a great many people who didn't speak English were able to enjoy dancing and singing along to the lyrics of a U.S. hit single. They were moved by the energy of the music, not by any understanding of the words in the song.

When you're living your soul purpose, you can impact people you don't even see or know. The only limitation on your impact is your vision. If you're a musician, it may be your vision to play at concerts in your local area, or it may be your vision to secure a recording deal with an international music label. Your vision is yours to create, but it's important to realize that your vision is not your limitation. Your vision does not limit your ability to create a ripple effect that extends far beyond its confines. When you're living your soul purpose, you begin to connect with the souls of those you are destined to serve with your gifts, wherever they are.

Your vision can be revised at any time. Let's say your vision is to set up a business to serve your local geographical area. You may discover that you don't have enough clients locally to achieve your business goals, so you may decide to promote your business or open your doors to a global market by developing your business online. These changes and progressions represent revisions of your original vision.

When you're living your purpose and articulating it, there are no limits to your reach.

Your vision may change, but your soul purpose remains the same. Living your soul purpose allows you to reach out and touch the souls of others by being of service. Everyone has a soul, so when you're being of service, the only limit on the number of souls you can impact is in your own vision.

Changing Visions

Dr. John S. Pemberton had a vision of creating a new drink and selling it to customers at the local pharmacy, and in 1886 he did just that, giving his new drink the name of Coca-Cola®. What began as a vision of selling drinks to customers locally at five cents a glass has grown into a vision of quenching the thirst of the world with a drink that's now sold in over 200 countries. John S. Pemberton broadened his horizons, and the Coca-Cola Company of today now has a new vision that extends far beyond its origins in Atlanta, Georgia.

The Coca-Cola Company Vision:

> **Profit** – maximizing return to shareholders, while being mindful of our overall responsibilities.
>
> **People** – being a great place to work, where people are inspired to be the best they can be.
>
> **Portfolio** – bringing to the world a portfolio of beverage brands that anticipate and satisfy people's desires and needs.
>
> **Partners** – nurturing a winning network of partners and building mutual loyalty.
>
> **Planet** – being a responsible global citizen that makes a difference.
>
> **Productivity** – be a highly effective, lean, and fast-moving organization.

When people are able to use their gifts and use them fully, they are able to transcend in their vision. People who find their soul purpose, accept it, and then take steps to live that purpose will be successful in whatever they do. Abundance will be theirs.

Another great example of a transcending vision can be found in McDonald's, now a leading global foodservice retailer, but it all began with one drive-in Bar-B-Que restaurant in California. Ray Kroc was a multi-mixer salesman when he happened upon the restaurant in 1954. He found a restaurant that had been trading successfully since 1940, and its success had been built on providing a limited but quality menu. He had a vision for the business and pitched it to owners, Dick and Mac McDonald. His vision was to open McDonald's restaurants all across the U.S. In 1955 he founded the McDonald's Corporation and the rest, as they say, is history. Ray Kroc's vision for the business was quite different from the original vision created by the McDonald brothers, but the sole purpose was the same—to provide a consistently high quality service.

> *"If I had a brick for every time I've repeated the phrase 'Quality, Service, Cleanliness, and Value,' I think I'd probably be able to bridge the Atlantic Ocean with them."*
> —Ray Kroc

The stories of a great many famous individuals from all areas of life demonstrate perfectly how it's possible for individuals to transcend through their soul purpose.

Anita Baker

Anita Baker transcended from singing in her local gospel choir to becoming an international recording artist. Through her natural gift and being her own fingerprint, gospel music became mainstream.

> *"You leave home to seek your fortune, and when you get it, you go home and share it with your family."*
> —Anita Baker

Mo'Nique

Mo'Nique transcended from being a stand-up comedian in local comedy clubs to becoming the host of her own TV show and an Oscar-winning actress. As an advocate for owning your size and believing in yourself, no matter what you look like, her impact has inspired and empowered a great many women all over the world.

"I am a stand-up comedian who won an Oscar...
Oh baby, I did it. Me!"
—Mo'Nique, after winning her Academy Award

Eminem

Marshall Bruce Mathers III transcended from washing dishes in a restaurant and performing amateur rap at local venues to becoming an eleven-time Grammy award-winning international rap artist. By accepting his unique gifts and being his own fingerprint, Eminem was able to succeed as a white artist in a predominantly African-American industry.

"I am who I am, and I say what I think.
I'm not putting a face on for the record."
—Eminem

Eminem's story also demonstrates the point that your circumstances do not define who you are or dictate your potential to succeed. His troubled and impoverished childhood has been well-documented, but by recognizing and accepting his unique gifts, he was able to stand in his soul purpose, and abundance was provided. When times are hard and prospects seem limited, it's really important to find your soul purpose. When you recognize and accept your gifts and then stand in your purpose, success and abundance will come your way. Your natural gifts are all you need to elevate yourself above any kind of recession or poor economy. Your gifts may need to be cultivated in order for you to be of the utmost service through your purpose, but when you are standing in your purpose, the people and things you need will be attracted into your life.

For example, I once came across a lady who was a quilter. Quilting is a very old, traditional craft that has been passed down through many generations, but it's not a craft that's going to appeal to everyone.

The lady I met was extraordinarily skilled in her work, and her quilts were virtual works of art. When I stumbled across her, I had no real interest in the craft, and I thought that quilted goods were not really my thing, but the beauty of her creations inspired me to buy one of her pieces.

She had accepted her natural gifts and remained in her soul purpose, even though her craft may have been viewed by many as having only a limited market and, therefore, not a viable way of earning a living. By recognizing her unique gift and accepting and standing in her purpose, the people she needed and those she was destined to serve came her way. Her original vision had been to create quilted items that could be sold to support her local church, but she recognized that she was not using her gifts to the fullest and that she was destined to be of even greater service. She revised her vision and began to display her work to a much wider audience. Her work is now sought-after by people all over the world. Her only limitations were in her vision.

When you recognize your gifts and you use them fully to be of service through your soul purpose, you realize that fulfilling your purpose may take you way beyond your original vision. Barack and Michelle Obama could have settled and stayed still at any stage in their successful careers, but they would have been sitting in their purpose. It was their destiny to use their gifts fully and be of the utmost service by living fully through their soul purpose.

> *"Change will not come if we wait for some other person or some other time. We are the ones we've been waiting for. We are the change that we seek."*
> —President Barack Obama

Your soul purpose is your gift. Understanding that it's your gift and recognizing that it's yours to share by connecting on a soul level makes it possible to communicate it to the universe. We all have souls. Understanding the uniqueness of your gift allows you to identify the people you are destined to serve and then find ways of reaching out to them and sharing your gift. The more you can get out there and let people know about your gift, the more souls you can impact, and the greater the abundance for everyone. Knowing who you're destined to impact allows you to identify how best to communicate your gift to them.

Identify your tribe; identify the souls you are destined to serve.

When you understand your soul purpose and are willing to step into your abundance, it becomes business-like in that there are things you have to understand in order to make the biggest impact and the biggest ripple while you're here. This might mean writing and publishing articles about it or talking about it and presenting it in front of groups. It means finding ways to network and align yourself with like-minded people and organizations who can help you get the word out that you are ready to serve. Once you identify the right activities to help you, you have to then create an action plan and execute it.

When you're living your soul purpose, you have something really special. The more you feed it, the stronger you get and the stronger your impact will be on the world. You feed it by educating yourself through networking with like-minded people who can share their own experiences. When you find others who share similar gifts, they become a mentor for you as you learn how to communicate effectively and get your message out to the world.

For example, if you're a shoemaker, you may actually have inherited your gift from your family, but you're living in a changing world, and new shoemaking processes are developing all the time; new materials are being manufactured, new stitching methods, and new designs, and things may no longer be the same as when the business was started.

As a shoemaker, you need to evolve with the times, and educate yourself so that you are able to keep up with changing trends. But you also need to identify your uniqueness and develop ways to maintain that uniqueness as you move with the times. Your unique fingerprint sets you apart from all other shoemakers, and it's your uniqueness that will bring clients to you in the long-term. Educating yourself and feeding your soul purpose will allow you to continue producing the best end product possible. Take pride in being of the utmost service to the tribe that you're out there to serve. Broadening your horizons means keeping up with new innovations and also looking for new ways to tell the world about what you have to offer.

To broaden your horizons you need to...

- Identify your soul purpose
- Understand your tribe
- Understand how you can get in front of them
- Cultivate your soul purpose
- Identify ways to make the most of your gifts
- Provide the best service your gift allows you to offer.

When you're living your purpose and you're doing all of the above, you won't feel like you're working at it at all. You'll be happy to be doing it, and you'll feel passionate about it because it's what you're destined to do. If you're *not* living your purpose, everything is going to feel like hard work and, try as you might, you're not going to be successful in the things you do. There are going to be times when you *are* living your purpose that you will face challenges and meet difficulties, but the difference is that when you're doing what your gift has destined you to do, the people and things you need to help you find a way through, over, or around those challenges *will* come to you. You *will* be successful.

There might also be times when you feel that you are in the right place, but you don't have the right momentum. For example, your client base may not be growing as fast as you had hoped if you're embarking on a new business venture, but it's not that you haven't identified your soul purpose. It's an indication that you need to look for ways to build your momentum by strengthening your impact and expanding your reach.

When you're living your purpose, you feel energized. If you're working at something that's not your soul purpose, you will not have the same source of energy. You may know what your soul purpose is, but find yourself working at something you know is not. This might be because of pressure from outside sources, a spouse or partner telling you that you "have to get a job" to pay household bills. When you're not fulfilling your purpose, you will not feel motivated by what you do, and ultimately, you will not succeed. It might take time to build your momentum in your purpose, but when you're living your soul purpose, you will be provided for.

Never give up when you know you are where you're meant to be.

To broaden your horizons, you must begin to look at people from a soul perspective, not a suit perspective. A person's outward appearance is irrelevant when you recognize that your gift has been given to you to impact people, not just white people, black people, U.S. citizens, or any other single group in society; your gift is for all people everywhere. When you're being of service through your purpose, you learn to identify the people who will benefit most from your gift; you will find the people you are destined to serve, and you will find ways to promote your gift, helping them to find you.

Your gifts can spread across the world. You may well begin to identify your tribe by looking at people from a soul perspective locally, but once you identify who those people are, when you see who it is you have been put on this earth to serve, you will realize that you can find those people all over the world. Your reach is unlimited when you're using your gifts to fulfill your soul purpose.

**Your soul purpose is love,
and love transcends all things.**

Thomas' Story:
A MASON WITH PURPOSE

What I See When Looking at a Rock

It's not what I see when I look at a stone or a rock.
It's what I'm reminded of,
What vision comes to my mind,
And that vision is my husband, a master stonemason.
I've come so much to appreciate his energy,
His love,
And his essence of being that he has shared with me.
So not only will the stone and rock work that he has
created last forever,
But so will the love I have for him.
No one can take away the memories which are
imprinted in my mind
From the life we have shared thus far.
—Donna Tickannen-Davis

I am the fourth oldest child from a family of 10 children, and I grew up in a family that emphasized responsibility in terms of contributing to the family as a group. I learned from an early age that there was a certain level of input or involvement that was required, or desirable, and through that I learned to take responsibility for my own process of learning within the family. I had plenty of guidance, but I was left to develop my own ways of doing things within the group. I think that was very advantageous in my early life and also in helping me find my soul purpose.

When I was about 16 years old, my mother asked my neighbor to give me a job to keep me out of trouble. He was a Scottish fellow named Robert Malcolm, and at 6 feet, 8 inches tall, weighing around 275 pounds without a bit of fat on him. He had a huge physical presence, but he also had a huge personality. He was a very folksy, down-to-earth, traditional man, and everything in his life was influenced by what his father, his grandfather, his uncles, and his great uncles had done before him.

He was a stonemason, and his work was like his homage to them, the tribe he'd come from, as 10 generations of his family had been stonemasons in Scotland. The origins of his craft and his whole philosophy had been passed on to him, and he instilled in me the importance of the precision and skill in his work and the need to have patience to be able to do what he did and what I now do today. He was a perfectionist who demanded a lot of me as an apprentice, but he also returned a lot to me. He always explained why he wanted things to be a certain way, not only technically, but also from an artistic and a traditional perspective. Through him, I realized the true reward of doing what I do, of being able to stand back after completing a job and know that I've created a thing of beauty that will still be there long after I'm gone.

He had a whole level of expectation that I strove to attain, and I think that's probably the real source of my discovery that what I do is what I was meant to do.

Robert lived alone because his family had passed away. His only son was killed in an auto accident when he was about 30 years old, and his wife had already passed five years before. He was in the latter years of his career, having been forced at the age of 72 to retire from his work, which involved traveling around Michigan, building various stone buildings from local materials. He wasn't ready to retire, so he went on to work for a local general contractor who focused on pools and landscapes. I worked with him as an apprentice for nearly four years until, in my fourth year, he passed away.

When he did, he left me pretty much everything he had, and certainly everything related to being a stonemason and to what we had been doing together. He left me his tools, his books—many of which were very rare—and a huge amount of material that allowed me to continue my education toward a European Guild Craft qualification. He also left me his connections, and I continued to work with Ron Steffis, who owned a company creating pools for the entertainment industry. At the time his clients included big names in Motown, such as Aretha Franklin, the Temptations, and Marvin Gaye. Ron wasn't a stonemason himself, and he wasn't even a landscape architect, but he had a great vision of stone around moving water, and most of his pools were just that.

After Robert passed, Ron became a mentor to me and continued to give me the work I'd been doing with Robert. He also set me up financially with any other tools I needed to get my business in place and become efficient in my everyday work with him. He was a great mentor artistically for me, not only because of his own vision, but also because he always treated me as an artist rather than a construction worker.

My work is a representation of my own being.

Ron saw the skill I had, and he was the first person to put the idea into my head that what I did would last far beyond my lifetime, and because it was a representation of my own being and my own self, I could never actually leave anything I considered to be less than my best because it would always be there. He confirmed Robert's belief in the importance of detail in what I did and also in running a business. I felt driven to always leave behind the best I could do visually and artistically and the best I could provide as far as functionality and quality. My work had to be something that said good things about me rather than something I wasn't proud of.

After four or five years, Ron died in a plane crash. His brother and son took over the business, but within months, they drove it into bankruptcy, with some of my money in their pocket, I might add. This was my first bad experience of business, as I realized that all of my eggs had been in one basket, and I had been focused on working only for them. Their bankruptcy meant I had to start again, so it gave me an opportunity to step back and question whether it was really what I was supposed to be doing. I was about 25 years old at this point, and it was a critical point in my life.

I had to question if what I was doing was what I wanted to keep doing and if it really was my soul purpose.

It wasn't a difficult question to answer because I was good at what I did, I enjoyed doing what I did, and it was really rewarding. There was a good return on it, and when I walked away from a job, I always felt really proud and satisfied that I'd created something that was beautiful and lasting and that pleased my clientele. I knew it was what I wanted to do, but I still had to decide how to go forward from where I was.

I had a thousand flyers printed that said a little about myself on them, and I went out into the Detroit neighborhoods that I thought could use my services. I literally went door-to-door dropping my flyers. As a result, I got calls. I started with mainly small repair jobs, but within two or three years, I had to decide what was next for my business. To go for bigger projects, I would have needed to take on a partner, but I knew I didn't want to become the executive driver of a business. I wanted to *do* what I did; it was an artistic outlet for me, so I opted to stay as I was.

Things grew, mainly through word of mouth, and I became recognized for doing what I did after a couple of projects got some local press attention. A director of Henry Ford Estates called and asked me to take a look at some restoration work. Working there gave me greater exposure, and through that I received multiple restoration projects at the University of Michigan, which was built on land bequeathed by Henry Ford. They were projects that gave me more media exposure and helped to raise my profile and establish my reputation as a restoration expert.

I connected with my tribe, and they began to seek me out.

At that point, the business was starting to take care of itself in terms of knowing where my next project was coming from, and I was starting to hook into my tribe, the people who really valued architecture and the sensitive treatment of it. They were now seeking me out, and this led to my getting involved in some larger restoration projects, through which I became part of a restoration team. In the '90s, my business grew again as new housing developments began to use more stone in their construction. Now, my business revolved around new housing projects as well as restoration work, and I started to get calls from architects and contractors who wanted me to do stone projects on their clients' homes. This meant I was working within the industry through contractors again, and I rode that wave until 2006, when things pretty much came to a halt as the bottom fell out of the housing market.

My business dropped by around 60 percent, so once again I was at a crossroads.

I had to take another good look at what I was doing, why I was doing it, and question if it was time to do something else because I still had a mortgage to pay! I made the decision to go back to where I'd started and reassert myself with old clients by letting them know I was still around and doing what I had done for them in previous years. I began to build my clientele again in the same way I originally had, but this time I knew I needed to take it in a different direction. I had so much more experience and had kept on educating myself and staying on the edge of what people were doing with stone, so I re-established myself with my original tribe and also reached out to new clients by looking for ways to create work that would be seen publicly, not just privately. This meant getting involved in sculpture parks, volunteer work, community installations, and community-sponsored art projects.

My tribe includes the people who see me as an artist; those who are not part of my tribe see me as a construction worker. My home highlights not only my craft skills, but also my design skills. It's a reflection of who I am and also a reflection of my wife's flair for color. It serves to remind me of what I have to bring to my tribe and the importance of what I have to offer, along with the responsibility of having to maintain the quality of my work in everything I do.

I'm aware that my tribe is a certain socio-economic group; they are people who have the means, the freedom, and also the perspective to see my work from an artistic point of view, but they also understand the functionality of what I create. They are people who have achieved success themselves, so they are able to step back and appreciate what I bring to the table. Of course, this doesn't mean all of my projects revolve around my tribe; day-to-day work still has to be done in order to pay the bills. I've had both big and small jobs through the course of my career. When I first started working, I had a lot of small projects, but as my journey went on, I also had jobs worth over a million dollars.

When I meet with a new client, they come into the relationship with certain expectations. It's my responsibility when we first meet to establish what it is they want and then to map out the process of how we're going to get from where we are at the beginning to where we want to be at the end. It's my responsibility to educate them to a degree and also help create a vision they can understand, a shared vision. Some clients already know my work, so after the first meeting, they step back and hand it over to me. They don't question any of the processes; they just wait for the end result, and they trust me to produce what they want. On the other hand, those who don't know my work so well but know what they want and think they know how to get there might need to be taken with me on my journey toward my vision so that they have a level of comfort in being taken step-by-step toward an understanding of my vision, even if it's not a vision that's shared immediately. It's my responsibility to help build their level of trust in my vision for them.

I feel inspired by stone, and I pick up energy from stone.

It's important for me to share my knowledge with others and pass on my skills to anyone who is ready to take on the challenge. It's not so much an intellectual challenge; it's having the patience to learn and develop a great many skills, but anyone who wants to do it can do it. My focus has always been on doing the best I can in whatever it is I'm doing at any moment in time. Always doing my best right then and right there — living in the moment. I don't always know where my next project is coming from, but I know that by always doing my best on the job I'm doing, I'm setting the wheels in motion to create the next job. I know I have to keep raising awareness and keep finding new ways to connect with my tribe and to let them know where I am, but I focus on doing my best on the project I have, not worrying about where the next one is.

When you live your purpose fully, what you need will come to you.

Thomas Davis
Master Stonemason
Custom Mason Contractors Inc.
www.stonemasonconsultant.com

CHAPTER EIGHT
LOVE WHAT YOU DO

*"Choose a job you love, and you will never
have to work a day in your life."*
—Confucius

WHEN YOU'RE LIVING YOUR SOUL purpose, you feel passionate about what you do and have an energy about you that radiates from you and lets people know that you love what you do.

When I was first starting out on my journey, I spent a lot of time traveling and visiting different companies. I worked with them to identify their challenges and helped them find ways to accomplish their goals. It wasn't until I was talking to a family member about what I did in my job that I realized I was doing something other people might find exhausting. They felt they could never work on such a hectic schedule, yet I had never thought about how much I was doing because I loved doing it. The extensive travel and long working hours didn't feel like work because I was living my purpose, and everything that came along with that was worth it.

Interestingly, that same family member who felt she could never do what I did now owns a successful performing arts school where she works with children to prepare them for the world's stage—now that's something *I* could never do!

Your natural gifts can make doing the things you do seem effortless, but living your soul purpose can still be demanding. When I was starting out with my day spa business, I had a lot of paperwork to take care of and documents to procure, but I also had to be the receptionist on a daily basis until I could put the right staff members in place. I owned the business, but I was working on reception, preparing refreshments for clients, cleaning the premises at the end of each day, and taking the laundry home with me because I didn't have facilities onsite. I had trained staff members who provided the treatments, but I had to take care of everything else in the early days. It *was* exhausting, but I didn't want to be anywhere else. As the business grew, I was able to install laundry facilities onsite and hire a receptionist so that I became the manager. As the business continued to grow, I was able to hire a manager, and then I was simply the business owner. It *was* a lot of work in the beginning, but it didn't feel like work because I was living my purpose; I was providing a service to the community by creating a relaxing environment and a safe haven for people to enjoy, so my passion drove me. If I had *not* been living my purpose, I would not have had the energy or the drive to continue working under the same demands. Every day would have drained me, and I'd have ended each day feeling like I had cement boots on my feet. Every little thing on a daily basis would have been a real effort.

When you're living your purpose and sharing your gift, you become energized. The universe will give you everything you need to be effective, so if you're living your purpose, you're not going to go hungry. You need food to sustain you, allowing you to continue sharing your gift, so the food you need will be provided.

However, this doesn't mean you'll always be in a position to eat well. When I became bankrupt, I ate whatever I could afford with the few dollars I was able to find, but the point is, I *was* able to find those few dollars to eat. There were times when I didn't know where I'd find the next few dollars, and then friends who didn't know about my situation would invite me to lunch or dinner. When you're living your purpose, things like that happen. I didn't always know where it was coming from, but the food I needed to sustain me was provided.

At a time when I had nothing, I was taken care of.

We can learn a great deal about the abundance of love from the story of Jesus in the Bible. Jesus wasn't a millionaire, but He always had food to eat and a place to sleep. The people He needed came to Him, and wherever He went, He was always ready to serve. What He needed was provided, and through His love, He was able to provide for others. In the "Feeding of the Five-thousand," also known as "The miracle of the five loaves and two fish," (Mathew 14: 15-21) Jesus was able to feed a multitude of followers with only five small barley loaves and two small fish given to Him by a boy.

When you're living your purpose, everything you need will be provided, but it's worth noting that there's a distinct difference between the words "need" and "want"! Often what they think they need is really not a need at all; it's really just something they want. It's a reflection of our culture that a great many things that are, in fact, luxuries, are considered to be needs. For example, let's say you're laid-off, and you don't have a job. You are still able to be of service, but because you don't have a job, things seem upside-down. My advice to anyone in this position is to go and find a place where you can be of service. Look for places where you can volunteer your services and be involved in something you feel passionate about. If you're passionate about children, volunteer to work in a charity shop that raises funds for causes related to children; if you're passionate about animals, volunteer to help out at your local animal shelter or rescue center. When you get involved in doing something, whatever you need will show up. When you're doing something you feel passionate about, the things you need will begin to come your way.

> *"Don't aim for success if you want it; just do what you love and believe in it, and it will come naturally."*
> —David Frost

History shows us that it's often in times of recession that the best businesses are built. Inspired business ideas are often the result of being stripped bare of everything you had in terms of material possessions, leaving you with only your natural self. When this happens, you become free to discover the essence of who you really are, and you are free to just be yourself. What could be perceived as a loss is actually a gain when you are given the opportunity to reconnect with the very essence of your being.

Entrepreneurs born out of recession...

Hewlett-Packard – *a company born in a garage at the end of the Great Depression.*
Microsoft – *founded by Bill Gates during the 1975 recession.*
Dyson Vacuum Company – *launched by James Dyson during the depression of the early 1990s.*

People who stood firm in their purpose...

Walt Disney *was fired by a newspaper editor because he "lacked imagination and had no good ideas."*
Fred Astaire's testing director at MGM wrote a memo saying, "Can't act. Can't sing. Slightly bald. Can dance a little."

Henry Ford failed and went broke five times
before he succeeded.
Elvis Presley was fired after only one performance at the Grand
Ole Opry, being told, "You ain't going nowhere, son.
You ought to go back to drivin' a truck."

I know a number of people who worked for many years in corporate America, only to find it was becoming laborious. This doesn't necessarily mean they've been in the wrong place all that time. It's more often the case that the jobs they've been working in have helped them cultivate their gifts, so being there was a part of their journey toward fulfilling their soul purpose. The amount of time you spend in a job and the energy you feel when you're in that job can be likened to the changing seasons in nature. When seasons change, you feel a change of energy. When your energy changes in your job, it marks the end of your season there, and it's time to move on to the next one.

I've been in jobs where everything was just fine, but I came to realize that I was only destined to be there for a short while. I was in those jobs for a reason, and that reason was not only to give and be of service, but also to gain something I needed to move closer to my soul purpose. When that gain is accomplished, something you may not realize at the time, the environment then changes. Your reason for being there may have been to pick up a skill, impact someone you may not even have been aware of, or have someone impact you in some way, but when that's accomplished, the tides can change. The change of environment should not be taken personally. It's not a case of changing from being good at your job to being bad at your job. The change of environment is only an indication that it's the end of your season there; it's a signal that you've grown enough to move into the next one.

Indications that it's time to move on and that you're not in your soul purpose include:

- Heart palpitations; a feeling of being anxious to move on.
- Feeling heavy every morning as you get up and get ready for work; hitting the snooze button on your alarm over and over!
- Dreading going to work.
- Little things at work that may normally have gone unnoticed begin to get on your nerves.

If you're not in your zone, if you're not meant to be there, it's not something you should view as a bad thing, but it is something you must recognize and act on. You must take steps to move on. When it feels like work, it's not your soul purpose. When you're standing in your soul purpose, you will still be working, but you'll be so passionate about what you're doing that it won't feel like work. Moving on might mean setting up your own business and working for yourself. In most cases, people working for themselves will work far harder than if they were working for someone else, but they will feel energized by what they're doing because they're doing what they're destined to do. When you're working for someone else, especially in a large organization, you generally have only one aspect of the business to focus on, but when you're starting your own business, you need to have an understanding of every aspect of your business. The demands can be greater, but you will feel energized by the experience.

Martin Luther King, Jr. had an intense schedule, but he was living his soul purpose. His passion and energy allowed him to work tirelessly. Living his purpose didn't mean it was all smooth sailing. He had opposition, but he understood his soul purpose and was able to stand firm. He stood in his soul purpose and remained passionate until the very end. His impact is still rippling across the universe several times over.

When you love what you do, you will...

- Initiate getting the energy you need to do what you do really well.
- Jump out of bed in the morning already thinking of other ways you might serve.
- Anticipate what you need to do to make a difference.

When you're living your soul purpose, you're passionate about it, so you share your gifts with other people. You're driven, but not in an egotistical way, to look for ways to help others. Your mind is divine, and whatever your gifts are, the things you need to help you make use of those gifts and serve your soul purpose will come to you. When you know that those things are coming your way, you're open to receiving them, and you're also open to recognizing what you're destined to do next at each stage in your journey. You recognize what it is you need to do and you work at it every day, but it feels right.

If you're living your purpose, your everyday activities might be interrupted by having a heavy cold or spraining your ankle, but you'll still feel that you want to do something even if it's limited to working at things in your mind. When I became aware of the need to take greater care of my health, I took action to find a personal trainer. It was important to me to maintain my health so that I could continue to serve my purpose, but my knees and ankles began to ache, so I had to find other ways to work at my fitness. Not being able to stick to the program devised by my trainer didn't stop me from moving forward; I just had to find alternative exercises. When you're passionate about doing something, you become unstoppable.

It's always easier to do what you're inspired to do than what you feel obliged to do.

When you're doing what you're destined to do, resistance will still show up, but your passion drives you through it. When you're living your purpose, the way around blockers will come to you, but when you're not living your purpose, the same resistance or blockers become excuses to stay still or give up completely.

A lack of acceptance can also be a potential barrier to moving forwards. Seeking the acceptance of others can become another excuse for stalling or giving up, but not everyone is going to understand your gift or your purpose the way you do. When you *know* you're doing what's right for you, when you love what you do, you already have all the acceptance you need: self-acceptance.

You might have the gift of a beautiful singing voice and share your gift by performing on stage. Not everyone in the audience is going to receive your gift in the same way. Some will cheer and applaud appreciatively, some might be moved to tears, and others may sit in their seats and only applaud out of politeness. People are going to respond differently to what you have to offer, but you know you are out there on that stage to be of service to your tribe, and when you're doing what you love, the only acceptance you need is your own.

Your friends and family are not necessarily your tribe; they're not necessarily the people you are destined to serve, so they're not always going to recognize your gift the way you do, no matter how passionate you are about it. Friends and family who love you will be happy that you're passionate about what you do and that you're energized by it, so whether or not they "get" what you do is not important.

Your soul purpose is connected to love.

When you love what you do, you are able to understand real love. When you're living your soul purpose and you're connecting with others on a soul level, you're able to recognize and love your real self. When you connect with what you love, you learn to recognize that same real love in all aspects of your life.

When you love what you do, it's not work, it's love.

Staying Connected To What You Love

- Stay connected to the people and things that inspire you.
- Create positive affirmations.
- Stay healthy. Make it possible to be your best and do your best in whatever you do.
- Laugh. Find and spend time in environments that lighten your spirit.
- Cultivate your gift; educate yourself. Get to know what's going on in the universe. The more you know, the better you can serve your purpose. Your gift is a gift to the universe.
- Give back. Maintain the flow of energy by giving back to the universe, and the universe will provide everything you need to continue doing what you love in return.

Willis' Story:
A LEADER WITH PURPOSE

"You inspire your team by working as hard as they do, and when you don't, they don't feel they're being led by a real leader."
—Willis Cantey

I was born in Columbia, South Carolina in 1974. I have two younger sisters, and I spent all of my childhood there before leaving to go to college at the University of the South in Tennessee. I then moved to Panama, where I worked for a financial services firm for about a year. That firm turned out to be a bunch of crooks! I left to come back to South Carolina, where I went to the International Business School at the University of South Carolina.

I got my master's degree there, and following graduation, I worked for Xerox in Argentina, eventually moving to their headquarters (HQ) in Connecticut. After about nine months, Xerox was basically going to lay off everyone in my entire division. Although they offered me an opportunity to move to Rochester, New York, I passed. Instead I went to New York City and started to work for an Internet start-up company. This was 1999, and I had three great years there because everything was new, and I had to wear a lot of different hats.

Being laid-off was possibly the best thing that ever happened to me.

However, I knew I wanted to go back to South Carolina, and I returned to work as leader of a development team before moving over to a consulting group where I ran a professional services team. At the same time, I had a side-business and ran a painting and yard crew. We renovated houses, which I then rented out. I discovered that I liked running my own business so much that I was really creating jobs for myself so that I could keep doing it. I realized that this was something you can't achieve in a big company because unless you're really running the show, you're just one of many. This prompted me to leave and start my own business.

Before you can start your own business, you have to be ready to take a risk. When I first moved back to South Carolina, I wasn't ready, and I took a job because, frankly, working in a big company is safe. In a big company, you might get laid-off, but it's safe because there are healthcare and other benefits. You get a raise for doing a good job, and at the end of the year you'll keep your job. When you start out on your own, it's scary because you're giving all that up! In employment, you do what other people think is the right thing to do, and if you do a good job, you get moved up. However, while running my own business, I do what *I* think is right every day for the sole reason that it's what I think I should be doing. I no longer need to justify myself.

I took the risk.

An opportunity presented itself, and I bought a small existing business. It was a very small IT firm that employed only two people. It was not doing well, so I bought it for a nominal sum. I took the risk because I reasoned that when you're in employment, you take your last paycheck and that's it. There's nothing residual; whereas, with my own business, I had options. I could sell it or hire someone else to run it, so I saw more upsides than downsides to taking the risk. Risk taking was something I saw in other people who had already been successful, and this risk paid off for me.

I have more freedom; I don't have the worry about trying to make someone above me happy. I'm in charge.

Hiring people and giving raises are highlights of running your own business, but having to fire people or not being able to give bonuses because it's been a tough year are real low points, especially when you know people need the money. It's hard, but you really do have to learn to live with that. When you hire people, you have an obligation to them. The people you hire put their trust in you, so you've got to be a leader, and you've got to be confident. When you hire someone, it's not just a negotiation about salary. It's a career move for these folks; you have to question whether you're giving them an opportunity to have a good career. When all is said and done, I'm the one who has to apologize to a client when a project gets messed up, and I'm the one who has to tell an employee when things are just not working out.

There *are* tough times, but there are also rewards. We provide IT support, and when people call us, it tends to be a fairly serious situation—my Internet is down, my email is not working, I lost a document, I think the server crashed. We can fix these problems, which is rewarding, but it's also high stress because when people contact us, it's always urgent, and that wears on you. When we can't fix issues as quickly as the client would like, that can be uncomfortable for everybody, but when you're working with technology, it can be tricky—sometimes technology really is a magical thing! Another reward is that we've bought our own building now, and we're having a lot of fun with that. But, perhaps, the biggest reward is that I do what I want to do, when I want to do it, and there's great freedom in that.

Sometimes the highlights of running my own business are looking back and reflecting on all that we've achieved. We started with three of us sharing an office, and now we have our own building. We can look back on the first time a server crashed, and we didn't know how to fix it, and through that I can see just how far we've come. The income statement is really just a numerical pat on the back. Being happy with what I've achieved and recognizing how much we've grown as a company and how much better I've become as a manager or leader are almost bigger rewards than anything else.

When I work long days, it's because I'm building something for myself and for my team.

I believe that you have to lead by example. I can't ask people to work late all of the time if I'm going to leave at 4:30 every day. I can't ask my team to work on the weekends if they know that I would never do the same. You inspire people when you work as hard as your team, and when you don't, they don't feel like they're being led by a real leader. My wife of five years is a great support to me, and she knows more about business than I do. I like to get her involved whenever I can. She is very involved in her family's business and has a lot of first-hand experience, so I look to her for advice on a regular basis.

I take more vacation time than I used to, but I probably work just as many hours. I think about my business more than I did before, but it's exciting! With technology, there are always new things, and if I think businesses are going to be using Macs more in the future, I don't have to justify that thought to anyone. I just gather my team and say we're going to start training on Macs. I love that freedom to do what I think is right. When I go away for a week, I know the company will continue to run well because of the standards we've put in place. I can step back and the business will still run. It becomes independent. It's my goal to, at one point, become the owner and less of a manager of a business, to become more strategic and less tactical, and we're getting there.

It took years, but my team shares my vision for the business.

My team members are all very good with computers, but they're also all very good with people. That's something we work hard on all the time because social skills are just as important as technical skills in our business. I can teach someone how to work on computers, but I can't teach someone how to be gracious with clients.

I know what I'm looking for in a prospective employee, but I also bring my wife and office manager in on hiring decisions because they have skills that allow them to see other characteristics that I may miss. For example, they can gauge what they call the "creep factor," and I can't! I want everyone—men and women—to feel comfortable with the person I hire because they may be going to people's homes. I can't figure out everything; the technical guys know more about someone's technical abilities than I do, so I need everyone's input.

I hire people who have been doing the job for at least 10 years, so I don't spend a lot on training because they have already been trained. This means that when someone calls the company, they will always speak to someone who is experienced, and they won't be passed from person to person.

Clients see us as a professional business. When they call, they always get a friendly answer, and they're never left trying to hunt down the right person or waiting for someone to call them back. They also know the person they're talking to will understand if they feel the conversation is getting too technical. It's all about meeting the needs of each individual client and not throwing out information they don't need to know. We're a business with organization and hustle, which are vital when you're competing for clients every day. Our responsiveness allows us to grow, and it's something that clients like. Of course, we also fix problems, and that's why they hire us.

My ideal clients are people who are not looking at my team as just salespeople; they're looking at my team as people who can give them information and educate them on the newest and latest technology available. They see technology as an advantage, and they want to be at the cutting edge. However, we also work with clients who view technology as an expense, and they need cost-effective solutions to problems. We cater to everyone, and the clients we attract are looking for the unique combination of computer *and* people skills. We're not the cheapest, but we come up with the best solution to solve *their* particular problem, and they put their trust in us to do that.

It's important in business to be able to adjust and wear multiple hats over the course of the day, and having people skills is critical to the success of my business. One client might be detail-oriented, and another not interested in being given any details; they just want me to let them know when it's fixed!

A lot of things can only be learned through experience; there are a lot of things you're not taught in business school. You learn them only through being in business.

I think sometimes people hesitate even when they see what they need to do in life because that something doesn't represent a *big* idea. It's important to realize that it doesn't have to be a big idea. Your idea doesn't have to be something you can put a patent on. We're doing the same thing that thousands of other people are doing, *but* we're trying to do it better.

Looking back, I knew in high school that I wanted to situate myself in a position in which I'd get a lot of interaction with people. In school I enjoyed being part of a team or group, and I was someone whom people liked to get behind. I'd run for office and get elected and be surprised, but then I'd run again for something and get elected again. I realized it was something I was able to do and something I could build on, but I didn't fully understand how until later in life.

If I was to go back and do it all again, I'd probably do what I'm doing now sooner.

Perhaps the right opportunity came at the right time, but I could have done what I'm doing now years ago. If I had not hesitated, I'd probably have a bigger business today. I had a great experience as an employee, but I knew I was going to be a small business guy. By moving around from country to country and job to job, I learned how to adjust to new cultures and make new friends. I think these experiences helped me to grow into my soul purpose.

Willis Cantey
President, Cantey Technology
www.canteytechnology.com

CHAPTER NINE
GROWING INTO YOUR PURPOSE

"You have got to discover you, what you do, and trust it."
—Barbra Streisand

IMAGINE IF YOU WERE LIVING your soul purpose and monetizing it. How much more money would you make than what you're making now? People who are living and monetizing their soul purpose find fulfillment in addition to profit because they lead a balanced life. If you aren't implementing and monetizing your soul purpose, you will make some money, but you will not be fulfilled, and your earning potential is affected. Your quality of life is much lower because you aren't fulfilled. Monetizing your soul purpose is part of growing into it.

When you are growing in your purpose, you understand what that purpose is and who you are here to serve. When you have that understanding, you are able to identify ways to be the best you can be through your purpose and be of the utmost service.

By continuing to grow in your soul purpose, you continue to make the most of your gift and can keep offering your tribe the best service you possibly can by making full use of that gift. By growing in your purpose, you maintain the flow of energy that will bring abundance to you and to your tribe.

Growth is ongoing and often begins before you are fully aware of your soul purpose. For example, let's say you are a young woman who is still at school, but who has learned the power of self-acceptance and the value of just being herself. You are someone who can confidently stay away from the drug culture that surrounds many of your peers, and through your ability, demonstrate alternative ways to have fun as a young woman. You are able to influence other young women and encourage them to follow the same path. You are someone who has recognized the value of your uniqueness and is naturally in the midst of those you are destined to serve, but as a young woman, you may not yet have recognized this as your soul purpose. As you mature into an older woman, you begin to grow into your purpose as you start to understand your gifts and recognize your ability to empower other women. You grow into your purpose by recognizing it and then strengthening your impact by broadening your horizons and extending your reach.

**As you grow physically
and emotionally,
you also grow into your purpose.**

Many people who identify their soul purpose as adults look back on their experiences in life to realize that their gift was always with them, even in early childhood. Professional singers have often been singers from childhood; dancers have been dancers from childhood, and great organizers have often been demonstrating their organizational skills since childhood. When they learn to recognize their gifts and identify their soul purpose, they are also able to recognize that their gifts have been growing with them, and they have grown into that purpose.

> *"You are today where your thoughts*
> *have brought you; you will be tomorrow*
> *where your thoughts take you."*
> —James Allen

Growing into your purpose allows you to identify ways to become more effective and strengthen the impact you have through your purpose. The more you grow, the more influence you have, and the greater the ripple effect you're able to create as you serve your purpose. For example, someone who grows to become a peacemaker will be a peacemaker, no matter where they go in the world. They may have grown from being a child in a large family with many siblings who could find ways to keep the peace in a crowded home to being someone who can find ways to promote peace in areas of conflict around the globe. As you grow and mature physically and emotionally, you grow into opportunities to step up to your purpose and leverage your gifts. Someone with calm reasoning ability may grow into a lawyer or a counselor, someone with decision-making and negotiation skills may grow into a politician, and someone with technical skills may grow into an engineer. The growth then continues, as each individual finds ways to develop their skills and become the best they can be in whatever they do.

Your soul purpose is something you are born with. Your gifts have been given to you exclusively. As you grow as a person, you grow into fulfilling the needs of the people you are here to serve; you grow into fulfilling the needs of the universe at any given point in time. My soul purpose is to be of service to others by helping them to live their own soul purpose fully, making the most of their unique offerings. I've worked in many different environments and with a wide range of people, and my gifts have grown with me in everything, from delivering newspapers, to working with Fortune 500 companies, to growing my own business to six figures.

When I was growing up, I wanted to do my part to bring additional income into the family home. One of my first jobs was with McDonald's, and I realized then that by working there and being of service, I gained a great deal more than just money. The opportunity to be of service and provide the best service I could gave me the opportunity to develop my gifts and grow into my purpose. I then worked in hospitality in a hotel, and although my reason for being there was to earn money, I once again gained much more by being in a position to look after the needs of other people and provide the best service possible. After college, the jobs I then grew into as an adult made full use of the skills I'd already developed through being of service and understanding the needs of other people.

At Microsoft I was able to approach each company with an understanding of what the unique challenges were for them in their particular industry. Being of the utmost service meant being able to see the company from their point of view and understanding what was and was not of importance to them. To me, being of service meant being able to identify the things that would be of most value, and consequently, that would add value to the company before I even got there. Each job on my journey provided me with further opportunities to develop the gifts I had been born with and to grow more into my purpose.

Your growth does not stop when you reach the point of identifying your soul purpose and who you are here to serve. Your growth continues as you learn to recognize the transformation your gift creates in those you serve and the impact that serving your purpose has on the lives of others. For example, you may be a gifted singer as a child and grow to recognize that your singing voice has an impact on the people around you. You then grow to recognize your voice as your gift and begin to strengthen your impact by broadening your horizons and singing to a wider audience. As your reach extends, you learn to recognize who you are here to serve by recognizing the transformation your gift provides. You then grow further into your purpose by seeking more ways to share your gift and bring the same transformation to others.

You grow as you begin to realize how much your gift is appreciated by others. It may be that you grew up with a natural ability and willingness to help your grandparents, and that grew into a natural affinity to older people and a desire to be of service to them in any way you could to enhance their lives. Something that came naturally to you becomes something you feel passionate about, and the energy you give to those you help is returned to you through their appreciation. The flow of energy generates further growth as you look for ways to be of even greater service in something you love to do.

If you are living your soul purpose, the more you continue to grow, the more your confidence in who you are and what you are here to do also grows. As your confidence grows, you become able to stand firm in your purpose, and by standing firm, the power of your influence and the strength of your impact also grow.

If you're gifted and blessed enough to be living your soul purpose and to feel the love that living your purpose brings, you must honor it by cultivating it and actively looking for ways to get better at doing what you do and offering what you have to the universe. This might mean enrolling in training courses or simply doing more of what you do in order to hone your skills, but you must continue to move forward in order to continue growing in your purpose.

You are the best at being you. Be even better.

You are already your own unique fingerprint and no one can do what you do better than you, but by continuing to grow, you become even better at doing what you do. Growth is essential to ensure that there are no limits placed on your ability to go on living your soul purpose and to live that purpose *fully*. Living your purpose fully may take you to a place that is way beyond your current reality and perhaps even beyond the limits of your imagination, so you must continually grow, keep pushing those boundaries and make your possibilities endless.

> *"If we did all things we are capable of,*
> *we would astound ourselves."*
> —Thomas Edison

When you recognize and accept your soul purpose, you also accept the abundance your purpose will provide. The more you grow into your purpose, the greater that abundance becomes. As you live your purpose and grow in it, you continue to make room in your life for all the good things that are coming your way by letting go of the people and the things that are not supporting your purpose. There can be no limits placed on the level of influence you can have when living your purpose and, therefore, no limits on the abundance your purpose will provide for you and for those you are here to serve. By continuing to grow, you ensure you're placing no limits on yourself or those you serve.

Growing into your purpose can also be thought of as expanding your purpose. Another way to expand your soul purpose is to help someone else to live their soul purpose fully. By helping them to grow in confidence and make the most of their unique offering, you also continue to grow exponentially. The positive energy created through helping someone else, and the positive energy they then create by being of service in their purpose, increases the flow of energy returned from the universe.

"The blossom vanishes of itself as the fruit grows. So will your lower self vanish as the Divine grows within you."
—Vivekananda

SECTION TWO

ACHIEVING RESULTS: SOUL PURPOSE IMPLEMENTATION

THE SECOND SECTION OF THIS book is intended to show you how to implement your soul purpose and live it fully. You have to explore your purpose before you can learn how to implement it, but once you start living your soul purpose, you'll see everything fall into place.

Sometimes through life's ups and downs, it's easy to lose confidence and begin to doubt yourself, but when you are positive that you're living your soul purpose, nothing can stop you from finding success. These chapters set out a step-by-step process that will help you regain your confidence and learn how to truly live your soul purpose using everything that's available to you.

CHAPTER TEN
UNDERSTAND YOUR VISION

"A vision is not just a picture of what could be; it is an
appeal to our better selves, a call to become something more."
—Rosabeth Moss Kanter

THERE IS NO LIMIT TO what you can accomplish. It's simply
a matter of how you formulate your vision. When you understand
your soul purpose, you understand your destiny in terms of why you
are here and who you are here to serve by using your gifts.

Now you must create a vision based on that understanding and on
how comfortably you're standing in your purpose. For example,
your purpose might be to enhance people's lives through art. When
creating your vision, you need to focus on the form of art you feel
most passionate about. Let's say that your particular niche is the
architecture of Paris. Your gift is the gift of art, and your unique
fingerprint is art depicting the buildings of Paris. You now know
that your tribe is going to be people who appreciate art, beautiful
buildings, and are interested in Paris, so your vision is your view of

how you're going to share your gift with the people you are here to serve. Your vision might be to share your passion in your home area by displaying your work in local art galleries; it might be to share your passion nationally by displaying your work in galleries across the whole country; or it might be to make your art available to a global audience via the Internet. However you see yourself sharing your gift, that's your vision.

Your gift has been given to you so that you may use it to be of service to others. I encourage you to think big when formulating your vision. Everyone's definition of "big" is going to be different, but it's important to challenge yourself to think in terms of how you might broaden your own horizons when creating your vision. This might mean thinking beyond your hometown to another, beyond your home state to another, or beyond your home country to another. But all of these ways of thinking represent thinking big for *you*.

The Frog in the Well
We think too small, like the frog at the bottom of the well.
He thinks the sky is only as big as the top of the well.
If he surfaced, he would have an entirely different view.
—Mao Tse-Tung

When you're structuring your vision, the sky is the limit. Along with an acceptance of your gift comes a responsibility to go out into the world to share it with others. If you're living your soul purpose, there are no limits to how far you can go, so the only limits are those you place on yourself in your vision. How far do you see yourself going?

Constructing Your Vision

Your vision provides you with tangible ways to measure your success. When you know and understand your soul purpose and who you're here on earth to serve, a vision of yourself living that purpose fully can begin to develop around your answers to the following questions:

- Where do you want to be five years from now?
- How far do you want to extend your reach?

Using the earlier example of an artist, five years from now her vision might be to own an art school that specializes in teaching architectural art. Her reach becomes global as the school offers residential courses to international students.

The more details you can add to your vision, the more powerful it becomes. For example, the above vision could develop further into owning a residential property with bedroom accommodation for six guests and a large internal space in which to create an art studio, along with a separate studio located outside in a three-acre garden area. More details could then be added, such as giving an exact location. Would you be in the inner city, suburbs, or a rural setting? What about the specific type of building—town house, apartment, or log cabin?

Further questions then need to be answered to develop your vision beyond what living your purpose fully will look like, in terms of using your gift to be of service and figuring out what making full use of your gift will bring you personally.

- What quality of life do you want to be enjoying five years from now?
- What lifestyle do you want to lead?

For our artist, quality of life might mean enjoying more family time by opening the art school doors to students for six months of the year and keeping the premises exclusively for private use and as a family residence the rest of the year. It might mean being able to travel extensively for three months of each year to fuel her passion by studying beautiful architecture all over the world. Her lifestyle may be one of attending a great many social functions connected to her art and growing notoriety in the art world, or it may be one of peace and tranquility, revolving around remaining close to her sources of inspiration.

There are no right and wrong answers to the questions. *Your* vision is *your* vision, but by taking time to construct a detailed picture of where you want to go and who you want to become by living your soul purpose, you make it possible to construct an action plan of steps you need to take in order to get you there efficiently.

> *"Vision without action is a dream.*
> *Action without vision is simply passing the time.*
> *Action with vision is making a positive difference."*
> —Joel Barker

Your vision must encompass all areas of your life. Create a vision of where you want to go in your professional life, whether that's embarking on a certain career path or achieving specific targets in your own business. Create a vision of where you want to go in your personal life, whether that's being able to spend more time at home with your family, take regular family vacations, maintain a fitness level that allows you to go on adventure trips all over the world, or devote more time to leisure activities and hobbies. There are no limits to what you can achieve when you're living your soul purpose, so it's important that your vision reflects the possibilities that are opened to you.

Five years from now, when your vision has become your reality, you will have created a more fulfilling life by encompassing every aspect. Without a clear vision, you may focus on one particular aspect while neglecting another, with the end result often being one of success, but not of fulfillment.

It takes a multi-dimensional vision to honor yourself and your soul purpose.

Never shy away from creating specific targets for yourself in your vision. More detail adds more power by providing greater focus. If it's your vision to extend your reach further around the globe, be specific about how you see yourself doing that. In other words, give yourself tangible ways of measuring your success. For example, if it's your vision to sell your product internationally, what would that look like? An outlet in one other country, in three other countries or in every country in the world? If it means three countries, which three countries? If it's your vision to become wealthy, does that mean having a million dollars in the bank, or does it mean owning properties to the value of one million dollars? If it's your vision to become a millionaire, *when* will you become a millionaire by?

If it's your vision to own a successful business, you also need to include details such as how many hours per week you will be working in the business and how many employees you will have. How will you know your business is successful? What will that look like? Your business must have a vision, and all of your employees must share that vision if the business is to be successful. Create a vision of who your employees will be. What will they look like, and where will you recruit them from? What will you offer your employees and provide for your employees to create a successful work environment? You must also create a vision of how you will reach your customers or clients—the people you are in business to serve. How do you see yourself communicating and connecting with your tribe? Advertising; magazine articles; Internet; books; demonstrations; exhibitions? What does success look, sound, feel, smell, and taste like?

Add color and substance to your vision.
Make it real.

A client of mine had a vast range of skills to offer businesses and created a vision of being able to provide those skills to multiple businesses as they needed them and being paid a retainer by each organization. Her unique offering was that she could provide small and medium-sized companies with skills that were essential to the success of the company without the company having to keep a full time person on staff. By being paid a retainer, companies could effectively budget for the use of her services. In her vision she identified the ways in which she would promote her services and spread the word to her tribe. She also set in place a system that would allow her to keep track of her appointments and work efficiently, as well as a back-up system to handle telephone calls at busy times. She saw her success in her vision, and in so doing, created her reality. By seeing exactly what her success looked like, she was able to take action to step into that success. She understood her vision.

> *A vision statement is sometimes called a vision of your company in the future, but it's so much more than that. Your vision statement is your inspiration...It articulates your hopes and dreams for your business. It reminds you of what you are trying to build. Let your imagination go and dare to dream...It's important that a vision statement captures your passion.*
> —Susan Ward

Virgin Atlantic Vision Statement

The success of our three-year strategy requires us to build on these foundations by focusing on the business and leisure markets and driving efficiency and effectiveness.

General Motors Vision Statement

GM's vision is to be the world leader in transportation products and related services. We will earn our customers' enthusiasm through continuous improvement driven by the integrity, teamwork, and innovation of GM people.

Toys 'R' Us Vision Statement

Our vision is to put joy in kids' hearts and a smile on parents' faces.

You need a clear understanding of your vision to have a clear understanding of who you are, what your gift is, and who you are destined to serve through your soul purpose with your gift. If you're not clear about what you have to offer or what you're going to do to spread the word about your unique offering, the people you are here to serve may not find you. The clearer your vision, the clearer your communication becomes with your tribe; the clearer your vision, the stronger your impact becomes on your tribe.

When you understand your vision, you understand what you need to do to support your vision and then turn it into a reality.

A clear understanding of your vision allows you to identify the most efficient and effective ways to communicate with your tribe and spread the word about what you have to offer. If your vision is to reach a global audience, an article in your local newspaper will have little effect. If your tribe includes young people under the age of 21, then giving a presentation at a senior citizens' afternoon club will have little effect. To communicate with your tribe, you must understand who they are, where they are, and the means of communication they are most frequently exposed to. Are they Internet users, newspaper readers, television watchers, or radio listeners?

> *"If you go as far as you can see,*
> *you will then see enough to go even farther."*
> —John Wooden

10 Guiding Principles to Living Your Vision Statement and Achieving Success

A vision statement can encompass all areas of your life. A vision statement of where you want to go in your professional life may include embarking on a certain career path or achieving specific targets in your own business. A vision statement of where you want to go in your personal life may include spending more time at home with your family, taking regular family vacations, or devoting more time to leisure activities and hobbies.

Here are 10 guiding principles for living your vision statement and achieving success in your career:

1. **Achieve your own success.** Whatever opportunity you choose to take, pick three things you want to accomplish within your organization. Pick things you know will make a difference within the organization, shoot high, and then stay focused on those things.

2. **Always be a professional.** Being a professional is not about knowing everything; it's about being credible. If you don't know, make a point of finding out, and then follow

up on the question. Always dress appropriately and look your best. When you're part of a team, allow others to take credit where credit is due; you don't have to act like you did everything.

3. **Keep texture in your life.** Don't set your sights on being a one-dimensional figure, and don't be too serious about your work. It may be your vision to be the best accountant in the world, but remember that people may prefer to be around an accountant who also enjoys cooking or music.

4. **Surround yourself with positive and forward-thinking people.** No one survives alone. Find yourself a mentor, and also be a mentor. Whether you are the mentor or the mentee, you will grow through the experience.

5. **Encourage, don't criticize.** Always look for ways to encourage others in their work. An individual may not be right for one particular position or department within the company, but that individual's skills may allow them to shine in another.

6. **Don't be over-technical.** Even when you work in a technical environment, always talk to people using appropriate language and avoid being over-technical. Tell your clients what they need to know, not what you know. It's not about the technology; it's about how the technology can improve their lives.

7. **Be an effective communicator.** Communication is key. Recognize that communication can be non-verbal as well as verbal, and develop your abilities to communicate effectively on all levels.

8. **Keep moving.** Realize there's no such thing as a setback. If it doesn't work out, move on to the next thing. Stay on the high frequency, not the low frequency, and understand that timing is everything.

9. **Live by principles.** The world is constantly changing. It's not always about the money or the promotions. In difficult economic times, a sideways step within a company can still represent progress as you develop new skills or gain the opportunity to help others to develop theirs. Consider volunteering in different positions to add to your skill set.

10. **Always be true to yourself.** Never sacrifice more than you can afford to lose. Always go with the things that keep you close to your purpose and who you really are. Your work should always be a win-win.

There is no limit to what you can accomplish; it's simply a matter of how you formulate your vision. When you understand your soul purpose, you understand your destiny in terms of why you are here and who you are here to serve by using your gifts.

> *"To understand the heart and mind of a person,*
> *look not at what he has already achieved,*
> *but at what he aspires to."*
> —Kahlil Gibran

Rod's Story:
A NURSE WITH PURPOSE

"Always take your standards forward with you."
—Rod Gamble

I was born to a 15-year-old mother in Arizona. She was a teen runaway, underage, away from home, and on the verge of getting married to a 19-year-old boy, so my arrival meant she had to grow up fast. She had hepatitis A and B, both of which she had received from my biological father, who was an IV drug user. The doctors told her to abort me because I would be born blind and retarded. But she didn't, and she provided for me as best she could, also providing me with a different dad.

Neither my mom nor the man I called "Dad" valued higher education—They thought of it as stuffed shirts and hot air—and they didn't think that real people who worked for a living went to college.

But I was a smart kid who always got good grades, so I knew it was something I was good at, and I decided that going to college was the right answer for me. Of course my parents had never considered that college was ever going to be an option, so they had made no provision for it and were surprised that I was taking that road. The challenge for me, therefore, was paying for it!

I was having to pay for college at the same time as I was going to college.

In the last few months of my high school career, I was trying to pull it all together, not knowing where I was going to go with it or how I was going to get the money to survive. I went to college, and though it took me six years to get my bachelor's degree, I own this achievement forever; it is mine.

I saw my mom violate certain laws, and consequently, she suffered many losses: her house, car, money, and retirement from the Air Force—she was kicked out after 19 years of service, only six months shy of having an income for the rest of her life. Having seen everything taken from her, I decided I wanted to create my own security, which could not be taken from me, and I saw an education as something that could never be taken away. I got a degree in nursing, partly down the same line of thinking because there are always going to be sick people. I was always going to have a job, unlike a job working in cars, electricity, or in a field where markets tend to go up and down.

Initially, I'd thought if I were going to go into the medical field, I should be a doctor. I was a pre-med student filling my requirements at the university, and one of the steps I had to take was to interview the doctors who were practicing the sort of medicine I wanted to practice. I didn't actually know what kind of medicine I wanted to practice, but I found some doctors to interview anyway! They all said the same thing, asking, "Are you in medical school now?" When I said I wasn't, they said, "Get out; medicine is not what it used to be; it's not good, and if I were you, I'd not want to be in this field 10 to 20 years from now. I think you should do something, anything else in the medical field, just don't be a doctor; it's not what it's cracked up to be or used to be." So at that point I had a decision to make. I wanted to take care of sick people, I had a bunch of college credits that were pre-med, and the most applicable choice from there was nursing school because I fulfilled all the prerequisites and was able to apply and get right in.

I made a number of observations when I was getting my nursing degree, and I also made a key observation on my first visit to the hospital to take vital signs. I was recently trained, so this was something new and exciting for me. I walked boldly into my patient's room and confidently took a set of vital signs, only to then realize that I had nowhere to write them down. I did what everybody does and took a napkin from the dispenser in the room and wrote on that. I then transported the napkin back to the nurses' station, transferred the information onto a graphic sheet, then wrote it in the chart, then on a clipboard that physicians would use to reference it. I also wrote it in a long hand part of the chart as well. When I was done, I'd written those vital signs five times for a single patient. I did the math in my head, realizing that if I were doing this five times for every single patient, it would mean that with every 20 patients or so, I was going to be writing 100 sets of vital signs. If I were extremely conscientious, I might mess that up just once, but which signs were going to be read? The 99 that I got right, or the one that I messed up?

The light turned on, and the scales fell from my eyes the first time I took vital signs.

At that point I was working nights for a customer service firm, and I had time on my hands to think about little technical problems

I needed to solve. I had begun writing databases and storing procedures, things of that nature, to do a lot of my work for me. I was able to do huge swaths of work in fractions of the time and had most of my time available for studying and catching up on my reading for nursing school. I put the two things together and decided that if I could do that for medical data, I could actually help prevent that one in 99 mistake from impacting somebody's care and causing them pain, suffering, or ultimately, death.

I realized I could make a difference with this little approach.

From that point forward, my nursing education was focused on automation, research, and the more technical aspects of the job. After that, I used my nursing degree to finance my computer science habit and as a way of formalizing my computer knowledge. Instead of having to be self-taught and learning everything the hard way, I was able to put my previous experience together with my education, allowing me to leap forward by learning the hardcore technical aspects from other people. I was lucky enough to have a master's coordinator who understood my area of interest and allowed me to focus my computer science master's thesis on healthcare systems and the various forms of programming techniques that would be appropriate to meeting the needs of a healthcare organization.

I graduated with a master's degree in computer science and found myself in a job market that had just gone bust. The dot-com era had come to an end; I was no longer able to walk out and expect to be paid just for being a programmer. That time was over for everyone, so now I had to look at doing something that put the two together. That something was working for a vendor of electronic medical records—Cerner, a healthcare technology information company— where I was able to put both the clinical and the technical aspects together in new and interesting ways, some of which hadn't been done before. I was working at a pediatric teaching and research facility, which was rather cutting-edge at the time, and I decided at that point that putting the two worlds together actually worked and was a viable career. I was able to use my technical training and preparation to advance my clinical beliefs.

I moved on from Cerner and refined my technical skills with a Fortune 500 company, but then came back to healthcare IT as a consultant with a unique solution set. I was able to provide solutions that met the needs of clients because I'd been down that road before. I knew the lessons they were about to learn, and I could give them a shortcut. This became the marketable side of what I wanted to do, and it has proved to be very marketable. Even during an economic downturn, I still receive multiple job offers each day.

I had known that I liked taking care of sick people and being in a hospital environment since the age of 15. At this age, however, an incident occurred that, though it shook my core, ended up being beneficial in the long run. My parents had me committed to a hospital because they believed I was an alcoholic after they found a bottle of alcohol in my car. At the time I didn't know that it was a common lie to say "I'm holding it for someone," but the truth was that I really was! I'd never had a drink in my life other than a sip of grandpa's wine, but they found it and came to the conclusion that I must be a closet alcoholic and threw me into Charter. Charter was an organization that worked with teenage alcohol and substance abusers, and the counselors there took about 12 hours to figure out I wasn't there for the right reasons. They were used to dealing with drug addicts and alcoholics, and I just didn't fit the profile. I wasn't one of the "normal" kids they were trying to take care of, so instead of focusing on rehabilitation, which wasn't needed, we focused on family dynamics. This was when I realized the power these people had to change people's lives, and also the real nature of my parents. Before then, I was really hating them, but after that experience, I could understand them more. I realized they meant well; they just didn't know what they were doing. I did not qualify to be involved with Charter, yet through being there, I came into contact with people who were able to help me see my life with more clarity. I wasn't there for the right reasons, but I still benefited from the help. As a 15-year-old, I leveraged the opportunity that had been presented to improve my relationship with my parents. I was able to change the family dynamics, and it was a pivotal time in my life.

I used what was essentially a bad situation to create a good outcome.

At first I thought I might like to be a psychiatrist or a counselor, but I came to realize it wasn't right for me. As I matured, the counseling aspect became less interesting to me, but the physical aspect of caring for people became something I felt more compelled to do.

A key mentor for me in nursing college was Dr. Kathy Jo Ellison. She was a real believer that nursing and computers belonged together, and she was a strong advocate for the use of computer technology in nursing together as one discipline. She told me that at some point in my career, I would need to make a choice between being at the bedside or being involved in computing, and she was right. Another mentor I had was a professor, Dr. Dorota Huizinga, who had a Ph.D. in education and computer science. She was very good at teaching, and it was through her that I discovered that learning is painful! This has since colored many of my experiences in life because whenever I feel myself being stretched, I wonder whether it's because I'm learning. I question if things are stressful because it's a bad situation, or if it's just because it's a new situation, and I use that to measure things in my life.

She told me that I had a unique combination of skills and that I should definitely work for no one but myself.

I think that was probably when the seed was planted in me to, one day, run my own business. However, in my family background, where you worked and who you worked for were the only questions ever asked, and the only other question to ask would be whether switching to another company might represent a better deal. There was never the paradigm of going out and getting the business yourself and deciding for yourself what was right. So, quite frankly, when Dr. Huizinga said that, it scared me. Motivational speaker Anthony Robbins teaches that fear and stretching are not necessarily bad things, and when you feel fear like that, you should reach out and pull for something you're actually capable of doing.

The thing that scares you is actually within reach. The fear is irrational; embrace the change.

So, at that point, I began to wrap my head around the idea a little bit. I didn't reject it because of other beliefs I had, but I didn't see a path to this change, or direction at all. It stayed that way until I began to work for Cerner, and I was able to see other people in consulting roles around me. I noticed that one or two of them worked for themselves. They were mysterious creatures who just came into my project, did the job the way they thought it should be done, made a whole ton of money, and then moved on in life. It seemed to me like they led a charmed existence, and I knew that I would also like to lead that charmed existence.

At the first hospital where Cerner sent me, I was told that I was going to fail there, but it was okay because the experience of failure could be a good thing, and they would then send me somewhere else. It was Children's Hospital of Orange County (CHOC), and the people who'd been in my position previously had lasted an average of six weeks. They were just grinding through people, and it was really due to the fact that they had a bunch of nurses working in the clinical IT area that were basically mean.

Nurses can be mean—it's common knowledge that, professionally, nurses eat their young—they're just mean to newcomers! Of course in that environment I was a nurse and I knew all about this behavior, so I was able to check it before it got out of hand. A year and a half later, I had not only survived, I was offered a great big promotion for my results. One of my VP's wanted to know how I'd managed to get results with a notoriously challenging client. I told him it was because of my nursing background, but I also knew it was because I knew who I was, I knew what I stood for, and I was able to come up with some novel solutions that really worked for them.

My confidence in myself came from a time when I was working as a registry nurse in Los Angeles. I'd been working in that position for two or three months when I was due to return to a hospital where I had once worked, but I was not looking forward to working there again. My first experience there was overwhelming because I found I had way too much to do. It would be the middle of the afternoon before I was able to check people's blood sugar levels the way I should have at noon, and I was left feeling that I must be doing a terribly bad job, until I noticed that some of the more senior nurses with years of experience behind them were in exactly the same boat.

I realized that we were all just twisting in the wind there.

Before going back a second time, I did a bit of research and discovered that if I rejected an assignment while working there, the worst they could do to me was fire me. Being fired is not the same as losing your license, so I went to work having made the decision that there was only so much I could do safely. When I was once again given ridiculous tasks that I felt jeopardized the safety of the patients, I refused to take responsibility for them, saying that if they were not happy with my decision, they could ask me to leave. It was terrifying the first time I did it, but by standing up for myself, I found that the nursing administration didn't want to send me home. Instead, they looked at the situation and backed down. I had to stand my ground and lay out my conditions many more times, but I was never sent home. I had nothing to lose by standing up for myself and everything to gain for myself, other nurses, and the patients by refusing to practice unsafe care.

I stood in my purpose of taking care of sick people.

Through that experience, I learned to bring my standards with me everywhere I went, and that by doing so, other people could benefit from them. I also acknowledged that I could also benefit from someone else's standards if they were higher than my own, and I'd learn from that person to take *that* standard with me.

I decided to quit Cerner when I grew tired of constantly traveling, and I went to work for Intel for a brief time. I was not in medicine at all in that position, and I was purely a computer programmer, using only the programming side of my brain—and boy was that painful!

I learned that I didn't really care about microchips and memory chips and all the rest of it and that I was completely out of place there. I realized that I needed to be back in healthcare. However, the side-step that Intel represented allowed me to work with and learn from world leaders in technology. I left there to begin working in a hospital in Santa Fe, New Mexico. The hospital was just up the street from my house, and it were on the verge of implementing Cerner, so it felt like a good move for me. While I was there, the hospital administrators remained undecided about signing the Cerner contract for about a year, so I worked on other systems such as Horizon, Per-Se, and other technologies for surgery. In my work I found solutions to the challenges they had with the performance of their systems, and this allowed them to provide better care for their patients.

I left that hospital to install electronic medical records at the physicians' offices, which were owned by the hospital at that time, and I set up many new systems from scratch. However, I actually did many things the wrong way for that project because I found myself being forced into bad decisions at that time by what turned out to be a corrupt leader. The corruption ran pretty deep, and when I became aware of it, I decided I couldn't be a part of it and left. The leader in question was taken away in handcuffs several months later.

It was then that I began to work as a sub-contractor on a number of projects until changes in employment laws led to the need to set up my own company. I became Rod Gamble, President of Gamble Corp.

Every step of the way through my stages of employment, I knew that no one, no matter what they said, cared about my career more than I did, and that, for me, is an entrepreneurial mindset.

I'm in charge, and I care about me more than everyone else. I'm also passionate about caring for sick people and helping provide the best care for people in the hospital. I take my standards forward with me in whatever I do. That's who I am, and that's what I'll leave behind when I'm gone.

My ideal client is a regional group of hospitals, small enough that decision makers are accessible by my consultants. They are the organizations who are open to bringing in experts who will help them to take better care of patients via the adoption of technology. The clients I attract are those looking to increase patient safety and efficiency. I'm known as someone who can ratchet up the overall level of quality so high and so broadly that everything else follows it. Clients find that by raising the level of patient care, higher profits and national recognition follow. I believe that quality leads everything, and by focusing on quality, you can actually change everything about healthcare. Part of that quality is increasing efficiency and delivery, and that's where technology comes in. Technology is just a tool to enable people who have real judgment and experience to function at their full potential. Technology provides gains both directly and indirectly. For example, reducing medication errors to less than one in 10,000 saves an organization an average of $34,000 per incident. Most facilities have an average medication error rate of eight percent, so you can do the math and figure out how much money each facility can save.

Documentation can also be improved to demonstrate the level of care that a patient has received, which sounds really basic, but yet, isn't. There are a lot of things that are done for patients that are not captured because it's simply too much of a pain to capture it—the documentation process is too lengthy and not always particularly related to the patient. But when you wrap the whole thing around quality in terms of high quality care and documentation, you become more valuable for those high quality services the patient receives while in the hospital. When the quality of care is much better, an organization can make money, save money, and make people healthier and happier. It's a win for everyone.

My ideal clients are not looking to be the lowest cost provider, but the highest quality provider, and they're willing to invest in themselves to position themselves as being the best in their region or territory. Healthcare is not Walmart; it's not about being the low cost leader, it's about being able to do the best job and produce the best quality care. To be able to do what I do, I have to be reimbursed appropriately. I have to be able to keep the machine running, and money is how I do that. In order to make a difference in people's lives, you have to be in business, and what you're doing has to make good economic sense and be competitive in the open market. If it doesn't compete, you're going to close the doors, and then you can't make a difference in anyone's life. You have to be financially liquid in order for things to flow.

Looking back, if I knew then what I know now, I would probably have stayed with my career in medicine and gained an M.D. because being a doctor would have given me a little more credibility than being a nurse. If I were going it all again, I'd also seek out more scholarship money to go to college so that I wouldn't have to struggle with that. As it was, I had student loan debt to deal with and work off, which was quite crippling at the beginning. Before going to college, my mom was thrown in prison for threatening to kill her commanding officer, which is when she lost everything. I still had a roof over my head for a while, but I ran out of money and lost a lot of weight because I didn't have enough food to eat. However, I never lost sight of my dream to go to college, and I still kept trying to look forward to how I could get myself there.

One of the benefits of living your soul purpose is knowing why you're getting up in the morning.

When you're living your soul purpose, you know that your decisions are already made. When you're faced with a new choice, you already have a set of values you can judge this particular choice against, so although it appears that you're making snap judgments, you're really not. You're just sharing the judgments you've already made with the rest of the world. It's also easier to be consistent in life because you know who you are already. I think monetizing my soul purpose is almost as important as living it because it's monetizing it that allows me to live it. I've made what I love to do into a career, and some days I can't believe that I get paid to do this. It's terrific! I could charge a lot less and still be happy, but I don't do that because I want to push my dream further. Monetizing it means you can do it every day. It's not a hobby; it's not the thing you do on the side. It's the thing you do full-time.

Your job is the most amount of time you spend away from your family, so therefore, it should be time spent doing something you love. I met my wife in seventh grade and asked her to marry me when we were 19, but she said no. This highlights a challenging aspect of knowing what you want in life because I knew I wanted her to be my wife, but she said no, and no one else was her! It was a dark time in my life, and I moved away to start my nursing degree. I was working nights to fund my studies, a good friend was stabbed in his sleep, and my younger brother had turned to drugs. It was a hard time, and it was difficult to see a way forward, but I just kept moving. Seven years later, my current-wife called to tell me she was ready, and we got married.

Today the culture of my company is one of open, positive collaboration. In fact, it's the very opposite of the negative reinforcement culture or shame-blame game that I dislike enormously. I enjoy a culture that's so open and collaborative that mistakes can be looked upon favorably because they represent a learning opportunity for everyone. That's who I am, and that's how I want to take the Gamble Corp. name forward. My core belief is to always be of service.

Rodney Gamble
President, Gamble Corp
www.gamblecorp.com

CHAPTER ELEVEN
CLARIFY YOUR VISION

"People are more inclined to be drawn in if
their leader has a compelling vision.
Great leaders help people get in touch with
their own aspirations and then will help them
forge those aspirations into a personal vision."
—John Kotter

TO CLARIFY YOUR VISION, YOU must be able to clearly identify who it is you are destined to serve when you are living your soul purpose. Clarifying your vision allows you to clearly articulate your soul purpose, which, in turn, makes it easier for your tribe—the people you are here to serve—to find you.

The more you understand your vision, the more you understand the different stages your tribe might be in. Understanding the stages allows you to identify the best way to be of service in each and every stage. You need a clear understanding of your vision so that you can make sure your tribe is clearly understanding your message. When you're clear in your message, you are speaking their language, and you are attracting them to your business.

For example, many of my clients are in healthcare in the U.S. and Canada, and one of the biggest offerings I have is that I'm able to bring administrators and clinicians together in order to make key decisions on what needs to be done. Then, we work through initiatives using the available technology to help get those things done.

Most of what I do falls into the category of patient safety, and when I am offering my services to large healthcare organizations in North America, I play an instrumental role in putting change into practice by bringing technology into an organization and bridging gaps between clinicians and non-clinicians. When I am clear about what purpose I am serving, I don't have any problem with organizations understanding the value I bring to them. By being clear, I automatically attract the people who are looking for a change agent who understands the healthcare environment, and by being clear, I can connect on all levels whether I'm in conversation with a CEO, manager, nurse, or clinician because I'm able to articulate what I can provide them.

Of course, if I talked to someone in a manufacturing company, I'm not going to attract them in the same way because they don't need what I offer; they're not looking for that service. That's the beauty of being clear. When I'm clear that I want to help health organizations get full use of healthcare reform and support them through the change with appropriate technology; then, I attract *exactly* whom I am here to serve. I help large healthcare organizations implement clinical applications and solutions to support patient safety and healthcare reform.

The challenges that healthcare organizations have and that I help them solve are the following:

1. Lack of agreement between administrators and clinicians to decide on the best solutions

2. Lack of clear communication regarding the value of implementing a solution

3. Having realistic and appropriate timelines to implement the clinical applications

4. Lack of appropriate measurements to track the effectiveness of the solution (before and after); how to ensure the technology truly improved patient safety

5. Lack of proper planning and proper inclusion of key stakeholders to make large implementations successful

6. Lack of guiding principles to keep everyone focused on the sole goal of improving patient safety through implementing clinical technology

7. Not being ready for the change that is guaranteed in large clinical implementations; Changes come in the form of processes, skill sets, technology, and sustainability

8. Getting a full understanding of what it takes to implement the solution

9. Getting buy-ins from clinicians

10. Putting the processes in place to ensure a quality deliverable

11. Understanding the expectations and timelines on how to meet ever-changing governmental regulations that significantly impact reimbursement

Knowing these challenges and understanding how to provide appropriate solutions has afforded me the ability to work with healthcare organizations all over the U.S. and in Canada.

There are certain TV commercials that air at certain times of the day with the intention of reaching their target audience, who is likely to be watching TV at that time. Let's say it's a company asking you, the viewer, "Have you been injured?" The message is clear. If you have been injured, they can help you claim compensation. If you are not injured, you're watching, but the message passes you by. If you *are* injured, the commercial comes to life for you. You are a part of the community that company is here to serve, and you receive a clear message about what they can do for you.

Clarity in your vision creates clarity in your message.

If I'm helping small businesses who are in the process of growing their business, I need to be clear about what it is I can do for them that will help them. To do this, I need to understand the challenges they're facing in their business at that point in time. It might be that I can help them increase efficiency, save money, or make more money by helping them to attract the level of business they need to make that money. If I'm clear with business owners and entrepreneurs who are facing challenges, they're going to be clear about what I have to offer them, and they're going to want to talk to me and learn more about my services because of that clarity.

When you're clear in your vision, you then have to be able to communicate it effectively enough to let your tribe know that you're there for them. In order to do that, you have to speak their language. This means speaking their language in terms of letting them know you understand the pain they're in or that you know the challenges they're facing. They need to know that you can offer a solution to *their* problems because you understand what those problems are.

You connect with them; you don't just offer a solution. If you offer a solution without addressing the problem, you will potentially miss your tribe because you will miss the opportunity to connect with them on their particular level.

Your focus must be on why the customer should buy the product, not the product itself. It doesn't matter how great your product is if the customer is unable to recognize its value in terms of *their* business. Approach your customers with a clear understanding of how your offering can help them address *their* needs and the needs of *their* business at *their* level. Their problem might be that it's taking them a long time to get their product out the door to their customer, that their market is being squeezed by increasing competition, or that the business is failing to meet the mark in terms of identifying what the customer really needs, so their product is being viewed as simply a commodity. When you approach each customer with a clear understanding of your vision, you are in a position to clearly articulate *exactly* what you can do to meet their needs because you understand those needs.

Being Clear

The benefits of clarifying your vision are:

- You attract the tribe you're here to serve.
- You attract the right people to your business, which equates to increased business and more money.
- You understand the different phases your community might be in and the different paths they may be on, so you understand how to be of the best service in each case. They may be failing, breaking even, or making money, but you can connect on all levels.
- You clearly articulate what you have to offer in a way that will attract your tribe to you. Your tribe will want to know more, and they'll be open to receiving your message and your offering.

Not Being Clear

The pitfalls of not clarifying your vision are:

- You become too general and unable to identify exactly who you're there to serve. For example, you might state that you're there to serve businesses, but which businesses? What size; what industry; what service; what product? When you're too general, you run the risk of not attracting *any* business because you haven't spoken anyone's language.
- You end up spending more money. You spend more in an attempt to attract more customers, but your message is too general to grab anyone's attention. It's more expensive to be vague.
- You are unable to identify or offer the levels of service your customers need in each phase.
- Your tribe will not understand your message. If people don't "get" you or your message, if people have to use their brains to really figure it out, they're not going to buy what you have to offer.

Be clear like a lighthouse to attract your tribe.

If they see the light, then they can get to you. If there's a fog, then there's no way to get to you and they might not even know you're there.

Clarifying your vision is a process. Once you understand what your vision is, and you are able to articulate your vision, you have the opportunity to then get granular and focused in relation to how best to serve your community and how best to solve the problems that are plaguing that community. Clarity allows you to get closer to the transformation you offer and show how you are going to provide that transformation. The closer you are, the crisper your communication becomes and the easier it is to articulate what that transformation looks like. It becomes easier to articulate how you can get your clients from where they are now to where they want to be, from facing a problem, to being on the other side of it with a solution.

For example, when people are looking for a personal trainer, they're looking for a transformation. The transformation may be to lose weight, tone up, get fit, or just to look fabulous, but the personal trainer represents the solution to getting from where they are now to where they want to be. If you are a personal trainer with a track record of helping clients lose an average of two to five pounds per week, you should be able to articulate that record and the fact that it's repeatable, so you can offer new clients the same transformation. Your tribe will include all of the people looking to lose that amount of weight at that rate. You are able to connect because you understand the problem they face, and you understand the transformation they want. As a personal trainer with that understanding, you are able to offer a solution to the problem, and with that understanding, your tribe members trust you to help them achieve the transformation they want the right way. You have to be clear about the transformation you're going to provide so that your clients can remain focused on that transformation, and not the sweaty workouts and change of diet that will be a part of the process!

By being clear, your clients receive a clear message that you are able to provide a solution to their problem.

To clarify your vision, figure out where you are now and where you want to go. Clarify how far you want your reach to extend. Do you want to reach your tribe locally, citywide, statewide, regionally, nationwide, or globally? Based on where you are now, you need a plan to get you from that point to the point you want to reach. This means identifying what the gap is and then identifying ways to bridge that gap. The gap might be limited funds, limited resources, limited help, or limited networking abilities. Once you've identified the gap, steps can be taken to bridge it by sourcing solutions.

Clarifying your vision also means being clear about the pace at which you want to move forward to the next level. Your vision may be to extend your reach globally, but based on where you are now, at what pace? You must also be clear about the kind of lifestyle you want to create or maintain as you move forward. For example, you might want to go global, but you don't want to be continually traveling because family time at home is important. This means being very intentional in your plan of how you're going to get from where you are to where you want to go. Your vision must hold true to what is most important to you as you journey forward.

To move forward you need to:

- Understand your vision
- Clarify your vision
- Be clear about how far you want to extend your reach
- Be clear about the pace at which you are going to extend your reach
- Ensure your whole lifestyle is being supported as you move forward

An important element of clarifying your vision is identifying how granular you need to be in order to communicate clearly with your tribe. For example, if your vision is to serve children all over the world, do you need to articulate your vision to the parents of the children, or to the children directly? Is your tribe the children, or the parents of the children? Who is the message for? In this case, it may be both of them, but you now need to be able to articulate your vision on multiple levels and across a wide range of age groups. Both the children and the parents of the children need to know what you have to offer and how that offering can solve a potential problem. You need to use language children can relate to in order to let them know that you understand their problem, and also language that parents can relate to, in order to let them know that you understand the problem and can provide a solution. In all cases, it must be language that clearly communicates an expected or desired transformation. Often, finding that language requires a testing process.

Let's say in this case, your vision is to help children learn through music. When you talk to the children, you're showing them how much music is fun. Their transformation is that they get to play music. However, when you're talking to the parents, you're not just talking about music; you're showing them the statistics and the case-studies that demonstrate the benefits. The parents want to know the value of your offering and its importance in relation to their child, so you have to test the best ways to communicate what you have to offer. To do this, you have to be clear about what it is *exactly* that you provide in the transformation; what's in it for them?

It might be that your transformation is the opportunity for children to learn without realizing they're learning. Learning is fun. Your offering is, therefore, of value to children with low attention spans or those who switch off in a conventional classroom environment. If you can communicate that clearly and clearly identify your tribe, your tribe can clearly identify you.

At one point I was working with a large retail organization that was facing challenges. The members of the organization understood their challenge to be too much inventory. However, their challenge was having the wrong inventory in the wrong place at the wrong time. To help them move forward, I began by looking for clarification on what, exactly, those challenges were. This allowed me to identify the need to keep merchandise moving as the main problem. They stocked clothing, and the general trend was that they needed smaller sizes in the southern part of the country and larger sizes in the northern part, but problems arose and opportunities to sell were lost as a result of stock not always being available at the right location.

The solution was to create a system that could track where the sizes were, what was being sold, and when it was being sold. The system made it easier to detect and follow trends, identify what was always selling or not selling, and to get the merchandise where it was needed. I had to understand the challenge first in order to find the solution. In this case, the solution was an improved, faster version of an existing system, highlighting that solutions don't always have to involve radical changes, just changes that add value.

Clarifying your vision is also important in personal relationships. The essence of any relationship is connection, and it takes a soulful connection to form a fulfilling relationship. However, visions of a relationship are often built around material things and things that have nothing to do with a soulful connection. A person's soul is not found in the car they drive or the clothes they wear; it's found in the characteristics that reveal who they really are, the characteristics that remain with them, regardless of the circumstances. Being funny, serious, ambitious, respectful, caring, or family-oriented are all examples of soulful character traits. When you're creating a vision of your ideal partner, always put your soul connections at the top of the list. The deal breakers shouldn't be having green eyes or driving a Mercedes; the deal breakers should only be the character traits that reveal the true person. This might be found in the way he or she treats other people or whether that person is a taker or a giver. These are the traits that will remain with an individual and won't change, no matter how much his or her external circumstances may change. Connect at a soul level and the only limitation is your vision.

Clarifying your vision is an ongoing process. Your vision can change and grow, so you must maintain its clarity at each new stage. Having guiding principles can help you with this. Your vision is supported by your guiding principles, so they can help you to remain clear in your vision and continue making the decisions that best support your vision. Decisions have to be made every day, but if you're always clear about your vision, you're always able to make decisions confidently.

> *"Clarity of mind means clarity of passion, too;*
> *this is why a great and clear mind loves ardently*
> *and sees distinctly what he loves."*
> —Blaise Pascal

Sandra's Story:
AN ARTIST
WITH PURPOSE

*"Sometimes we beat ourselves down and think that
we're not good enough to do something we want to
do... but until you're doing what you really want to
do, you can never be truly happy."*
—Sandra Bivins

I come from a family of 10 children, and I'm the oldest, so I was responsible for all my brothers and sisters until I got married and left home. My husband Arthur has been the love of my life ever since he gave me his bag of marbles. I have three children, two boys and a girl, nine grandchildren, and four great-grandchildren on the way.

When my husband was in the military, I worked in the officers' club in the dining room on the military base, which was wonderful because I was able to participate in all of the activities with the officers' wives. After he left the military, I had a security job in a department store and worked my way up to a better job.

I enjoyed my work, but I always knew that I wanted to be my own boss.

I never liked punching a clock and staying in one place for eight or so hours; I always knew I wanted to do something else. I *knew* that to be the case from a young age, but I didn't know what that something else was. After getting married, life became busy with other things and I never really thought about it while I was raising children, but after the children had grown and left home, I had time to think about it again and realize that something was missing.

I learned to quilt then, and that changed my perspective.

Quilting was something I'd always wanted to do, but the opportunity had just never crossed my path. When I was growing up, I went to the Salvation Army church and had the opportunity to stay at some of my friend's homes. I remember in one particular home I saw a beautiful quilt, and from that moment, I always wanted one. When my mother passed away, my sister gave me a box of things that had been hers, and inside it I found some quilts. I never realized that my mother had done any quilting. I'd always wanted to do it with her, but never got that chance. In fact, she had learned to quilt after I'd married and left home, but I never knew it. Sometime later, I was asked through my church to teach children and adults how to quilt, and that was when I began to learn the craft. I'd always had the desire to learn. I'd always been impressed by the work that went into it, but I just didn't know when I'd have the opportunity to try it myself.

As soon as I started to quilt, I knew what I was doing and it came naturally to me.

Through the church, the New Prospect Missionary Baptist Church, we started a quilting ministry. Before that time, I really hadn't realized that I had a talent for quilting, but now when I look back, I know that quilting was what I was *meant* to be doing, but it took all that time to find out. I had been good at my other jobs, but I knew I didn't like being stuck in one place all the time, especially when I was working in security. I'd go home at the end of a day's work with a bad feeling brought on by the events of that day. I was not fulfilled, and my employment was not feeding my soul.

Quilting *does* feed my soul. I can sit down at any time and pick up material, and everything that's bothering me is gone. I can look at anything, see a pattern in it, pick out the parts I like, and put them all into a quilt. I can go to the fabric store when I'm feeling down and upset or something's not working out and just by walking up and down the aisles and touching the fabric, I feel a sense of calm come over me. When I see pieces of fabric and how I can put those pieces of fabric back into a blanket, I really believe it's a gift that God gave me that I didn't know I had.

I had a gift; I just didn't know I had it.

Through the church quilting ministry, we made quilts for organizations such as nursing homes and hospitals, and we gave back a lot to the community in that way. When one of the two groups I was involved in split, I recognized it as an opportunity to do my own thing, but at the same time, I didn't feel that what I did was worthy of any particular interest. I didn't think I could go out on my own when I compared what I did with what some of the more experienced quilters I knew did. Some of their work was so detailed that when you saw it hanging up, it could have been a painting. I didn't feel ready, and it took me a while to walk away from the other group and to have the confidence to finally go it alone. I know now that I *am* ready.

There's no strife in quilting; it's like a sisterhood. I quilted with some great teachers, and I didn't see my work as being up to their standard. I was quilting, but I wanted to be able to do it better. It's a bit like learning to draw. My drawings were stick figures and theirs were much better, so I felt I didn't want to compete. The more you quilt, the better you become. At first I was most comfortable with African-American materials, and then I tried Asian materials and my confidence kept growing.

I'm now monetizing my purpose.

I realized that going it alone was something I *was* going to be able to do when I started showing my work in art galleries and getting a positive response, but I didn't realize that I'd be able to go as far as I have. I now know that I am where I'm supposed to be at this moment, and I'm working towards my future. When I first started showing, I thought of it as just showing, and it was the owner of the gallery who first suggested that I should display some prices on the pieces I was showing. At that point the people who bought my work were people I knew, so it was still a surprise to have people I didn't know express an interest in what I did, and an even bigger surprise to find that strangers wanted to buy it. I'd really only decided to show my work as a way of getting my name out there, and I hadn't really thought about whether I could sell what was on display. I was thinking in terms of the better you're known, the better you do.

Family is very important to me, and I made some wall hangers for my children that have family pictures incorporated into them. We've brought them up to understand the importance of each other and to always be there for each other because one day we won't be there for them. The pictures are there to give them a visual reminder that they still have each other to fall back on, even when mom or dad are no longer around. Quilting is all about bringing things together. It brings fabrics together, it brings quilters together, and it brings people together.

My vision for the future is to have my own gallery where I can hang my quilts and also have my friends hang theirs. I'd also like to teach my own quilting classes at the gallery. I've come full circle in that I learned to quilt through teaching children, and now I want to continue teaching by having my own class. To be able to do that, I need to enroll in some formal lessons myself because everything I learned was taught to me through other quilters. I need to study how to actually teach some of the basics that I simply picked up without realizing it. I'm always learning, and there's always something new to learn from other quilters.

Quilting is now and always will be part of who I am until I take my last breath. I'm hoping to teach my daughter and granddaughters, and I'm hoping that quilting is something that I will pass on to them. My granddaughter has tried quilting to please her mother, and my daughter has tried quilting to please me, but they're not ready to do it for themselves yet. I have materials set aside for when they are ready.

I would urge people not to wait as long as I did before doing something they know they want to do.

I love what I do and believe that had I realized earlier that this gift was within me, I could have been loving it more. Sometimes we beat ourselves down and think that we're not good enough to do something that we want to do, so we choose to do something else instead. But until you're doing what you really want to do, you can never be truly happy. I knew from a young age that I wanted my own business and to be my own boss, but even though I knew that, it took me a long time to act on it.

If you stumble, just pick yourself up and start again. It's okay to mess up. Sometimes I've messed up a quilt and had to start again, but the vision of what I want the quilt to be often becomes even greater the second time around. Through starting again, I gain a much clearer and often better vision of where I'm going with it.

It's just like raising a child. A child will stumble and fall and there will be tears, but you just have to pick them up and encourage them to give it another try.

I think one of the reasons I didn't move when I should have was that I didn't have a college education. I didn't feel that I could fit in with the people who were doing what I wanted to do. I thought I couldn't do it because of what I *didn't* have, and it took me a long time to realize that all I needed was what I *did* have. I had all I needed within me all along; I just didn't recognize it. I waited until my children were grown before I allowed myself to think about what I wanted to do, but I believe that you should not wait when you know what you are passionate about and what you are meant to do. The time is now.

Sandra Bivens
Artist
Art can be seen at Sherwood Forest Art
www.sherwoodforestart.com

CHAPTER TWELVE
CREATE A
PURPOSEFUL PLAN

"Strong lives are motivated by dynamic purposes;
lesser ones exist on wishes and inclinations."
—Kenneth Hildebrand

A PURPOSEFUL PLAN IS EFFECTIVELY a road map that can help you turn your vision into a reality. Once you have created a vision and you have clarity in that vision, you need a purposeful plan to get you from where you are now to where you are in your vision.

A purposeful plan helps you gauge your progress and your success as you journey toward living your soul purpose fully.

A purposeful plan provides focus and limits your potential to become sidetracked or distracted by things that are not supportive of your vision. A plan increases your efficiency because without a plan, there's a tendency to be reactionary instead of being strategically tactical in your approach to achieving your ultimate vision.

When you're fulfilling your soul purpose, not everything is going to go according to plan, and it's important to know that this is acceptable. Your plan may not always be exact, but your plan still allows you to be very intentional about how you are going to make a difference. It allows you to set the tone and set the stage in the universe regarding what you're trying to accomplish. For example, it may be your plan to reach 100 new people you are destined to serve in your first three months of providing that service, but as things work out, you reached only 30 people in those three months. This might seem discouraging, but the universe is out there to protect you and guide you toward being successful so that even though you didn't reach your target of 100 people in the first three months, that doesn't rule out the possibility that by the end of six months you might be reaching 200 or even 600 people with ease. A purposeful plan sets you on course to your success and, a bit like a barometer, helps you weather the storms and get back on track when things don't go exactly to plan.

To create a purposeful plan for your business you must...

- Understand your tribe; understand the community you are here to serve.
- Know what your financial goals are when operating your soul purpose.
- Know how far you want to extend your reach.
- Know the value of your products or services and understand their value as your offering to your tribe.

Having a plan allows you to sit down and work out what you have to do to achieve your ultimate goal and assess whether it's realistic from your starting point. A purposeful plan is a way of monetizing your soul purpose.

Sixteen Questions to Focus Your Purposeful Plan

To help monetize your soul purpose, try answering the following questions:

1. **What are your financial goals?**

2. **What services do you provide; what can you offer your tribe?**

3. **How many sales do you need?**

   To answer this question, you need to know your price point. For example, if you have a service package that costs $20,000 and you know you want to make $200,000 from selling the service package, you now know you need to make ten sales. Of course, to be able to make those ten sales, you may need to meet 110 people, but this is a process you can use with each service or product you provide to figure out the ratio of meetings to sales. If you are selling books online at $10 per item, and you want to make $10,000, you know you need to sell 1,000 books, but you also need to know how much traffic you need to bring to your website in order to make those 1,000 sales.

4. **What do you need to do to generate sales?**

   To answer this question, you need to identify ways to attract your customers, the people who will benefit from your service or product, and what you have to offer.

5. **How many people do you need to reach in order to achieve your financial goals and get what you have to offer out to your tribe?**

   You have a wide community to serve, and everyone is at a different point on their journey so never be discouraged by the fact that you may have to touch base with 20 people to be able to make one sale. You're still making a significant impact in being able to drive your soul purpose forward, and you're still making a difference, no matter what. Keep everything in perspective, and don't take "no" personally. Not everyone is in the right place to utilize your offering at the time you offer it to them. Be prepared to accommodate different scenarios. Some people will be in a position to pay in full, but others may benefit from a payment plan of some sort. They understand the value of your offering, and you know you can provide the transformation they want, so you may need to find a way to make what you have to offer accessible to them.

You can monetize your soul purpose, but it's not all about the finance, it's about your gift. What you have to offer is your gift, and it's a gift that is only yours. Only you can provide that service or that product in the way you are destined to do it. When it's your purpose to be of service, the money is going to come, but if you have a product set at a higher price point, work with your tribe to make it affordable. Keep the integrity of your price, but provide payment plans so people can benefit from your service or products. This doesn't mean intentionally putting yourself in the position of not being able to recover your funds; it means purposefully allowing yourself to provide a transformation by removing obstacles that may be preventing you from helping them.

Creating a purposeful plan is not something that applies only to business, but in all areas of life. Monetizing your soul purpose is always the end result because you need a sustainable income. The earlier you embrace your soul purpose, the earlier you provide yourself with the opportunity to live life to the fullest.

You may be a student, for example, studying for a career in communication. You still need a purposeful plan to help you achieve the end result you're hoping for. It may be your vision to be a TV newscaster, but you can begin to plant seeds while you're in school. While you're studying, you can be networking, attracting your tribe, cultivating your skills, and looking for opportunities to get you closer to fulfilling your soul purpose. This might mean looking for internships at your local radio or TV station, where you can begin to build relationships with other people who share the same goals. It also might mean practicing your skills by creating a video blog of interesting events in your life.

A purposeful plan allows you to practice and hone your skills, utilize your gift, and network with your tribe.

To be able to reach the people you are here to serve, you need to make yourself visible to them. Really get to know your tribe and be clear about the benefits they receive from your product or service; then, get to know the places where your tribe members spend their time and money. Identify no fewer than five places or activities that represent opportunities to make yourself visible to your tribe.

6. **Does your tribe include members of professional organizations?**

7. **Does your tribe include sports fans who attend games?**

8. **Does your tribe include business people who attend seminars?**

Identify the environment your tribe feels most comfortable in and consider creating that environment for them. This could be organizing seminars, workshops, or any activity that allows you to make yourself visible and let your tribe know you're there. When you know your financial goals, you know how much money you need to make, so you must now figure out how often you need to be at these places to attract enough people to generate that income. For example, you might get 20 people to attend your seminar, and out of those you may get five who sign up with you. If you know that you need 10 people to sign up every month, you know how many seminars you need to hold. Break your plan down from a monthly basis, to a weekly basis, to a daily basis.

When you have found ways to attract the attention of your tribe, you can then begin to convert interested people into people who are interested in partnering with you on the journey, people who want the transformation you offer. The next step is to plan how you will deliver the ultimate transformation to anyone who chooses to invest in themselves by partnering with you or your company and buying the product or service you offer.

9. **Do you need to schedule the delivery, or is it something that is instantly sent out after they sign-up?**

10. **How many times do you deliver it?**
If you are a service-oriented company, you only have so much time available, so how many deliveries can you feasibly schedule and keep all of your clients happy? Sales and delivery are equally important. If your service takes six weeks to deliver, you have that six-week responsibility. It's important to schedule time for delivery on sales already made and not just time for generating new sales.

11. **How many people do you need on your team?**

To be successful, you may need a team. You might be great at making sales, but not so great with the delivery.

Creating your purposeful plan is building a bigger picture.

As well as understanding what you want to earn, you must also understand what your personal investment will be in terms of delivering your offerings to your tribe. Break down what your investment into the business will be.

12.   **Do you need to invest in yourself to hone your skills?**

13.   **Do you need to outsource certain skills?**

14.   **Do you need a partner to increase your efficiency?**

15.   **Do you need to partner with another entity for effective delivery?**

16.   **Do you need to invest in your employees?**
      Figure out who you need on your team and also *what* you need in terms of essential items of equipment. You might know that you need to earn $300,000 in a year, but you might find that you need to invest $25,000 in order to realize that figure, or you may need to make an investment of time in order to see the 12,000 people required to generate that figure.

      Your plan creates a level of accountability to yourself, your team, and your tribe, so you need to break it down to that kind of granularity to be able to say, "Yes, I'm committed to this." Once *you're* committed, you share that by being clear about what you need from the people around you and sending clear messages to attract the right people into your business.

The people you bring into your team must support your own vision and fingerprint (cultivated environment or culture), and they must be able to support you in servicing your tribe. If it's your policy to have a big heart and be open and receptive to new ideas, you need individuals who value and share that policy, but if it's your policy to be very direct and to the point, you need people who share your approach.

A SWOT analysis—Strengths, Weaknesses, Opportunities, and Threats—can help you identify the needs of your business, but your team members need to represent your fingerprint. If you're an upbeat person and that's what attracts your tribe, you need the people who are rounding out your skill set to also be upbeat when interacting with your tribe. When choosing your team, ask yourself:

- Do they have the pertinent skills to do what's necessary in order to be successful in this role?
- Based on how much it costs to bring them onto the team, do I know I can get a return on my investment?
- Will this person bring what I need into the business?

When you're living your soul purpose, abundance will come. Your purposeful plan is how you plan for this. Your plan is how you materialize the abundance. When you are led by your desire to be of service to your tribe, the money will come. Things will not always go according to plan, and you will meet people who say "no," but don't be discouraged. A no is not a "no;" it's just that they're not ready for what you have, or they might not be a member of your tribe. The faster you get through the "no's," the quicker you get to the "yeses"!

Creating a Purposeful Plan

A purposeful plan is your guide toward living your purpose fully, and it's a way of tracking your progress. To help monetize your soul purpose, try answering the following questions:

- What is your financial goal for the year?
- What is the cost of your service or product?
- How many sales do you need to make to achieve your financial goal?
- How many leads do you need to generate that number of sales?
- How many leads do you need monthly, weekly, and daily to generate how many sales monthly, weekly, and daily?
- How many months per year will you work?

To answer these questions, you must consider your vision of the lifestyle you want to lead. Ensure that your purposeful plan supports your lifestyle.

"Make your work to be in keeping with your purpose."
—Leonardo da Vinci

Mia's Story:
AN ORATOR
WITH PURPOSE

*"When you self-connect, you make space in your life
to hear from your inner desires."*
—Mia Redrick

My professional background is in training and development, so for most of my career I was working with Fortune 500 companies, writing training programs, or actually being the facilitator for new training systems. Something I became aware of early on in my life was that whenever I had the opportunity to talk to groups of people, whether it was training, teaching, or a motivational talk of some sort, the results were always very good. It was something that came very naturally to me.

Back in high school, we were all required to take a speech class, and in a school-wide competition we all had to take part by doing a dramatic reading. It wasn't something that grabbed my interest, particularly at the time, but I ended up winning for my grade, then winning the school-wide competition, then the city-wide competition, and then the state-wide competition. I realized then that good things always happened whenever I would speak.

I didn't necessarily recognize it as a gift; it was just something that was there.

When I was younger, I just knew that when I was in a room full of people and I started to speak, they would listen and hear what I had to say. That was how I experienced it; it's like having a talent that you don't know you have. It's just there.

One of my first jobs was as a puppeteer. I was in an area of Baltimore that's popular with tourists, and people don't normally shop for puppets on a sight-seeing trip. Yet, I was able to sell thousands of dollars worth of puppets, just through being able to have a natural conversation with people. Another job was selling bolo ties, and again, people don't go to Baltimore to buy Bolo ties, yet I managed to sell thousands of them! I just always had a natural ability to communicate with people and be engaging.

I've always had a strong ability to communicate and connect with people, and I believe it's because I'm able to connect what I say with the listener in some emotional way. They may buy something; they may listen more; they may study more; they might be more excited; they might cry. Connecting is something I do well. I have an ability to take a message and share it in a way that helps people "get it." For example, children who have a disability or have had some form of emotional trauma may not be willing to speak to an adult, but they may be willing to talk to a puppet.

It's not just the communication or transaction of making a sale; it's how I connect with what I'm saying.

When I speak, I speak with a tremendous amount of authority, which obviously requires confidence, but there's something about me that means no matter what I'm talking about, it makes people want to listen. I'm passionate about what I talk about, and my gift is to be able to pass on that passion and communicate it clearly. I think people trust me. They know that what I say is what I mean, and when I say I'm going to do something, I'm going to do it. It inspires other people to join me.

For example, I took part in a mini-triathlon, and it was my goal to get 10 other moms to join me. Moms always think they're too busy to do things for themselves, so I saw the triathlon as a great source of motivation. I talked to moms about it and ended up with 23 moms joining me. I had not done a triathlon before, but I *decided* to do it. People get in on that, and they get excited about the transformation. They believe that I'm *going* to do it, and they *want* to do it, so we become a great team. That's what communication is all about.

People like me to be committed to their cause. If I'm there, I'm all heart, and I'm going to get in and get involved. People know that I believe what I'm saying, and when they hear me saying it, they believe me. It's their perception that it's the truth, and that's what they're drawn to. At one point I attended Toastmasters, and I loved the training and the processes. I would practice prepared speeches out loud as I had been taught, but then I'd go to deliver a speech, and *none* of what I'd carefully prepared would come out of my mouth at all! What I found instead was that my energy really came from the people in the room and the people I'd met before giving my speech. I'd find myself talking about what I'd learned from them and almost sensing what the particular needs of that audience were, and I would talk about those needs.

At times, speaking does feel very spiritual.

I think the spoken word is very powerful: I think you have to say what you mean, and for that reason, I don't watch TV because I'd rather influence my own thoughts. I trust myself. It was my mother who taught me to trust myself. She really groomed me to have high self-esteem because she did not have it and did not trust herself, but she instilled in me the belief that real power comes from the inside. In fact, I remember my mother reading *Pulling Your Own Strings* by Dr. Wayne W. Dyer with me when I was only 11 years old, and it stayed with me. I've never taken failure personally ever. My father always felt that real growth is in your imperfections, not your perfections, so I embraced that fact and have always felt comfortable with simply doing my best in everything I do.

What someone else did does not make what I did any less.

I was always willing to try to give it my best. I wasn't in competition with anyone, and I was always a confident, self-assured person. I always adopted an attitude of knowing what I was going to do, even though I really didn't know what that was! But once I knew what I wanted, I would communicate it, and then I wouldn't accept anything other than that.

When I was growing up, my mother supported me in anything I said I wanted to do. When it was time to apply to colleges, she helped me coordinate every last detail of everything I needed to have, everything I needed to do, and everywhere I needed to be so that I could go out and do it. I thought that was how it was for everyone until I realized that other people's parents were actually with them at the colleges. I didn't realize that my mother felt too intimidated to go with me. She made sure I had everything I needed, but, then, I had to go and do it. I had to get on the train and go to meet people myself. I was very secure, loved, and validated, and I knew when it was my time to be a mother, I'd be a great mother because of my own experience.

Something that has been an essential part of my life is keeping a journal. My mother got me to start when I was around eight years old. I wrote everything in there, and I didn't know that my mother used to read it so that she could counteract whatever it was she discovered was bothering me. She made me think independently by asking me to choose clothes that I liked instead of just clothes that everyone was wearing. She encouraged me to have friends from different worlds, so I had my school world, my extracurricular world, and my neighborhood world because inevitably, one of those worlds would crash, and if my entire world had been connected to that one world, I would have had nowhere to go and no safe place to fall.

There are always going to be things going on in the world, but it's how I choose to look at those things that makes the difference.

When I was in college, I had to take a class called ethics. It was a Catholic all-girls college, and they wanted me to say what *they* wanted me to say, but I had a problem with that. I felt controlled, in terms of speaking, and I rebelled, so I got a D. That was tough because I was used to getting great grades, and even though my friends all urged me to just say what they wanted me to say, I couldn't do it. I was an economics major, and I loved it. I was very good at it and got great grades, but I ended up with a teacher who really had "issues." I remember telling him that I wanted to be an economist, and he told me, "You won't do that; you can't do that." I felt at the time he was saying it because I was an African-American girl. He seemed to be determined to stand in my way and put me down. It really hurt me and made my time in his classes a real struggle. I was a confident young girl, but it was the first experience I'd had of someone trying to tell me that I wasn't unstoppable. He caused stress in my life, and I feel he abused his power by treating me the way he did, but he didn't succeed in stopping me.

When you stand in your purpose, you are unstoppable.

When I left college to start work at Citibank, I was young, and lots of people had been working there longer than I. So when I started moving up before them, they were not kind. In fact, they were negative. I could have folded in that environment because I was young, but instead, I decided to go to one of the vice presidents. I let her know what was going on and that people were sabotaging who I was; I was never afraid to share my story and tell it how it was. As it turned out, she promoted me and moved me to another area that was much more positive for me. That was my first experience of professional pressure, and I realized that even though you are really good at what you do, people can feel threatened by your being good.

I became a mom, but while I was still pregnant, my mom made me promise to date myself every week. A lot of moms lose themselves and their identity, so I joined a mom's group when I was six months pregnant. It was the best thing because it allowed me to build my support system *before* I needed it. It was like giving myself a head start because I had moms around me who already knew how to do all the stuff that was going to be so new to me. If I'd been hanging out with a bunch of other new moms, we'd all have been bumping our heads together!

I eventually became the president of my mom's group, and numbers grew rapidly. More and more moms came and joined, and it was at that point when I realized I had a gift. I *loved* being a mother; I loved being the president of the group; I loved being able to help other moms and saw the difference it made in their lives. I was able to share with them what my mom had shared with me. It was working, and it was a great testing ground for me.

When I had my first child, I told my husband I was going to go to work as me. My husband said, "I hope someone pays you for it!"

I realized I had two great things to offer: my ability to communicate, along with my passion to be a great mom. I listened to what people said, and they were questioning how it was possible to find the time to do all the things I was doing. Everything I was doing came naturally to me, but I found that five things were key in my life—finding time, finding meaning, connecting, personal growth, and focusing on my blueprint of motherhood. I knew I had to show other moms how to feel good about being a mom and not slip into just going through the motions. I wanted them to wake up in the morning and think, *Girl, you got it!*

I began coaching moms. I wasn't sure where my clients were going to come from, but I made the decision to do it. I told a few friends, and within a couple of weeks I had clients, perhaps because they already saw me as a center of influence. I then looked at coaching training, but I decided it wasn't really needed to coach moms, although it did offer a way to find structure in coaching, which allowed me to create a system that made it possible to share my gift effectively. I wanted something that was specific to moms because that didn't already exist.

I wanted to be able to help moms self-evolve, and I know that's what I'm here to provide.

I wrote my book, *Time for mom-Me*, which, in terms of monetizing my purpose, was a tool that was going to allow me to reach many moms, but keep me time-rich. My priority is being with my children, my family, and my husband, so the book allowed me to compound my time.

My tribe includes moms who want to be the best mom they can be by being the best they can be. I connect with my tribe through coaching, the book, and through an annual retreat which takes the form of a personal development cruise. It allows moms the time and opportunity to reconnect with themselves and do new and different things that push their boundaries. It's a way of challenging what they believe to be impossible and showing them how to make it possible.

Moms often have limiting beliefs. They can't imagine being away from their family for an extended period of time because they fear so many things—their husband might put their kids' clothes on backwards, and the world will end! I teach moms how to "feel" because they get so absorbed in being a mom that they can effectively become numb and forget how to feel about what they really want in life.

I feel I've been successful because while it's work, it doesn't feel like work.

What I do and what I get paid to do come naturally to me. It's like singing a song that you really love. It comes to me very easily. I enjoy it, and that's not to say that it comes without challenges, but the challenges are different from others I've had in that I feel I'm being guided along the way rather than pushing doors open all the time. After writing my book, I approached big organizations that I felt had the interests of moms at heart. Every single one of them contacted me personally within 48 hours. That's something that doesn't usually happen!

I've always had great ideas, and I've always been willing to share them, but I've now gotten smart about how to share them safely. Part of my gift may be feminine influence, but I've been able to take things full circle by passing on to other moms what my mom passed on to me. I've been able to monetize my passion and my soul purpose.

Mia Redrick
The Mom Strategist
Finding Definitions, LLC
www.findingdefinitions.com

CHAPTER THIRTEEN
IMPLEMENT YOUR PLAN

"For the things we have to learn before we can do them,
we learn by doing them."
—Aristotle

AS SOON AS YOU HAVE created a purposeful plan, that plan must then be put into practice immediately. Putting your plan into practice means putting it into action and into service. The steps to putting your plan into action can be summarized as follows:

Practice Operation Service Action

Practice – Operation

As soon as I have a purposeful plan, I immediately put it into practice by integrating it into my business operation, and I do exactly the same for my clients. Your purposeful plan is based on where your organization is, whether you're a start-up or you're established, and also where you are in your career or in your life. You now have to figure out how you can integrate your plan into your existing state. Your purposeful plan might be very gradual, but you have to identify how you're going to bridge the gap between having a plan and having a plan in action. Identifying how you're going to draw the bridge is putting your plan into operation.

Operation – Service

When you have a purposeful plan, you have identified your purpose and the purpose of your business, but by breathing life into your soul purpose, you rediscover how you can put your purpose into service. When you're living your soul purpose, you are being of the utmost service. This includes being of service to clients, customers, other businesses, and also within your own business. Putting your purposeful plan into service allows your employees to share an understanding of the plan and the spirit or intention behind it. By putting your plan into service, you're investing in yourself and your business.

Service – Action

When you put your plan into practice, operation, and service, you're applying it both internally and externally, and you're now ready to put it into action. Your purposeful plan will be broken down into yearly, monthly, weekly, and daily perspectives, so putting it into action is now doing what you have planned.

In some cases this might mean having to step backward before you can move forward. For example, if you're a nurse, and you want to change to a career in IT, you may need to retrain and gain some essential qualifications before you can make the change. Or you might leverage your clinical background and join a healthcare IT company or the IT part of your local healthcare organization.

In other cases you may need to look for ways to side-step into a new career. For example, if you're a teacher, and you want to get into corporate America, you may need to look for areas where you would be able to add value to an organization right away with the skills you already have. For example, you might look for fulfilling a corporation's need for trainers or working at corporations that serve educators or the education industry. Putting your plan into action means taking the necessary steps to bridge the gap between *knowing* what you need to do and *doing* what you need to do.

Putting your purposeful plan into action is like a circle that keeps going around.

You are constantly applying your purposeful plan, realizing the fruits of your work, executing your plan, and then instigating new ideas.

Apply Realize Execute Instigate

To instigate, you may find yourself in uncharted waters, but you must be prepared to provoke in order to take your business to another level. Your only limitation is your vision. There's nothing wrong with your current vision, but if you continue to instigate, you may come to realize you have been limiting yourself. When you instigate, you may be doing things different from how others do them. What you're doing might not be the status quo within your particular industry, but by offering a different perspective, you can provoke the status quo and promote change. What you're doing may be something people are not used to, but they're only not used to it yet. You might not fit into a perfect box, but the perfect box might not be there for you to fit into; you're creating your own niche. There's nothing like pushing the envelope in any area of life, but really you're not pushing the envelope, you're just being who you are. By being yourself, you're using your gift to be of service, and you may be providing that service in a form that people have not seen before. You become an agent of change.

You must always make sure you're holding yourself accountable. This means identifying what you need and who you need around you in order for you to do really well and to stay the course. It may be that you simply need to establish a routine that automatically provides you with room to reflect, feed your soul, and remain focused, but you may also need to recruit the help of others. If it's your plan to live a healthier lifestyle, you look to trainers and dieticians for advice and to be able to hold yourself accountable. It's the same when you're looking to live your life fully. You look for the people who can help you be accountable for being your best and providing the best service.

Leverage your support system; make use of the people who are supportive of your plan.

People who can help you to hold yourself accountable include:

- **Mentors** – Reach out for a mentor. Connect with people who are already living their soul purpose; learn from their insight and perspective to help you move forwards.
- **Coaches –** A coach is someone who can help you become the best you.
- **Advisors –** An advisor is someone who can advise you by providing additional knowledge, information, and experience.
- **Consultants –** A consultant is someone who can help you bridge the gap between knowing what your goals are and achieving them.
- **Mastermind groups –** Mastermind groups are groups of people who come together to provide support for each other by sharing experiences.

Who you need depends largely on your personal style and preference, but you need people who will support you in everything you do and help you to stay focused. Everybody needs somebody; it's very hard to do everything on your own. You have your vision and your way of providing your soul purpose, which will bring you abundance, but there are always ways to get better. To be better at being you and to be better at providing your best service, you need to have someone or something you can integrate into your life to make sure you're holding yourself accountable for making a difference. This is also something you need on an ongoing basis, which means that whether it's a good day or a bad day, you always have a way to pull yourself back and be supported in a positive manner, allowing you to keep on moving forward.

You should always take full advantage of people who can help you, and there's no reason to be doing everything alone or secretly. If you're there to serve a community, you need to be open and upfront about how you're going to be of the best service. Fortune 500 companies pay people to help them find ways to get better at what they do, so you need to invest in yourself to get the best out of yourself so that you can be of the utmost service. Athletes do it, world leaders do it, company presidents do it, and entrepreneurs do it; we're all students, and we can all be eternal students because there's always more to learn and something to improve on.

In the world of sports, athletes are supported by fitness trainers, performance coaches, sports psychologists, sports therapists, nutritionists, and a whole host of other support crew members. Getting to the top in sports, even solo sports, is not something an athlete can do alone.

Own the Podium

"Own the Podium 2010" was a national Canadian initiative supported by all of the country's winter sports organizations. Major funding partners, including Sport Canada, the Canadian Olympic Committee, the Canadian Paralympic Committee, and Vancouver 2010, designed to help Canada's winter athletes win the most number of medals at the 2010 Olympic Winter Games in Vancouver and place in the top-three nations in the gold medal count at the 2010 Paralympic Winter Games. Part of the initiative was to provide greater resources to the athletes-in-training in the form of trainers, coaches, therapists, psychologists, and nutritionists. Prior to 2010, Canada had hosted the Winter Games on two previous occasions, but had also become the only country not to have won a gold medal as the host nation. By pooling resources instead of each entity "going it alone," Canada not only won gold for the first time as the host nation, it broke the record for the most gold medals won by any one nation at a Winter Games, with a total of fourteen. The Canadian Paralympic athletes ended their Games with a total medal haul of 19, with 10 of them gold medals, making it their best result to date and placing them third on the medal table.

Executive Office of the President

In the world of politics, world leaders are supported by teams of advisory staff who provide them with essential information, making it possible for them to hold themselves accountable.

The Executive Office of the President (EOP) has traditionally been home to many of the President's closest advisors. President Barack Obama has advisors with specialized knowledge in subjects such as economics, the environment, national security, management, budgeting and administration, drug control, science and technology, energy and climate change, communications—including media affairs, research and speech writing, and economic recovery.

The EOP is a perfect example of recruiting help from the people you need around you to be accountable for your actions and be of the utmost service.

Companies always need to look for ways to communicate their ideas better, be of better service to their customers, clients, and employees, negotiate deals better, and be the best of the best. Continuing to learn and continually looking for ways to be better at being you and at doing what you do make it possible to be of the best service to your tribe.

Bridging the gap between knowing and doing has a lot to do with understanding your vision and clarifying what you need to do or where you need to go to be of the best service in your soul purpose. There can be times when you're fairly sure you know what it is you need to do but you're just not so sure of how to actually do it. When this happens, one thing you can be absolutely sure of is that you must keep moving.

> *"If you're not moving, you can't be directed along the way."*
> —Unknown

Just because you can't see exactly how you're going to do something, it doesn't mean you can't do it. Your plan does not have to be *perfect* before you can take action on it. You just have to be moving. Any action is better than no action. Sometimes people are unwilling to move because they want everything to be in place and perfect before they're willing to take that first step. People can sometimes be discouraged because they have a "perfect plan," but they're stuck because they're unsure of how to put it into action, or they've taken action and nothing is working out, so they think they have to toss it aside. These are all just challenges that we must face on our journey toward fulfilling our soul purpose. Getting there is not just knowing, it's also doing, and the challenge is to keep on doing. You just have to keep on moving. That's your doing.

Knowing does not guarantee that everything is going to be perfect. For example, you might know that your mission is to serve children in China, but if you are an African-American woman in the U.S., that might seem like the most outlandish idea. You know what you are destined to do, but you're not instantly going to know how you're going to go about doing it. However, you must embrace what you know and be open to receiving everything you need to help you fulfill your soul purpose.

I have a client who is a speech pathologist, and she knows that she wants to help children who are coming over to the U.S. from Asian countries. The children come from families who have made the investment to travel to the U.S., but they're not always able to articulate their level of knowledge and can often be misunderstood or overlooked. She knew it was her purpose, but who'd have thought that, as a speech pathologist in the U.S., she would have been able to be of service to this group of children? Her thoughts now are that if she can be of service to children of Asian countries coming to the U.S., she can also be of service to children from other countries who are coming to the U.S. and want to achieve the same success. She knows it's her soul purpose, but she doesn't yet know exactly how she's going to fulfill that purpose. There's no perfect plan of action in place, but she is already taking action to get there.

> *"First comes thought; then organization of that thought into ideas and plans; then transformation of those plans into reality. The beginning, as you will observe, is in your imagination."*
> —Napoleon Hill

When you're bridging the gap between knowing and doing, and you feel unsure, revisit the chapters in Section One and reconnect with your soul purpose. When you accepted your soul purpose, you had to take action to stand in that purpose, not sit, so you must now take action to implement your purposeful plan, not sit back and wait for it to implement itself. For example, if your purposeful plan says that this week you are to speak to two associations to try to get bookings, take action, implement the plan, and speak to two associations. Don't just plan; do. Even if your plan said make three calls, and you only make two, that's good. You're doing; *keep* doing.

Don't stop with the plan, don't stop doing. Keep going.

The Guru of Implementation

In my role as The Guru of Implementation, my clients count on me to guide them through the process of soul purpose implementation. It's my soul purpose to help others monetize their soul purpose, and the methodology for "Soul Purpose Implementation" never fails. It can be applied to any business, big or small; the results are the same.

A vision without a purposeful plan is as good as nothing.

Consulting with the Guru of Implementation allows clients to achieve the following:

- Identify the purpose
- Clarify the vision
- Design the purposeful plan
- Build the plan
- Take action
- Follow the plan
- Stay focused
- Expand their reach
- Hold themselves accountable

It's not good enough to know your soul purpose. You also have to build a plan and take action.

> *"I am so impressed by Melissa Evans, the Guru of Implementation. You may have great ideas, but you need to know how to implement them. She will show you how to take action."*
> —Hueina Su, The Nurturer's Coach

CHAPTER FOURTEEN
CLEAR YOUR BLOCKERS

"If you're trying to achieve, there will be roadblocks. I've had them; everybody has had them. But obstacles don't have to stop you. If you run into a wall, don't turn around and give up. Figure out how to climb it, go through it, or work around it."
—Michael Jordan

ALL OF US COME UP against potential blockers in life, and those blockers can stand in the way of being able to fully implement a purposeful plan. Anything that inhibits you or stands in the way of living your soul purpose is a blocker because those are the things that effectively block you from stepping into yourself. *Your* blockers are anything in your life that *you* perceive to be preventing you from living your soul purpose.

Blockers are *perceived* limitations. They are very often ideas that exist only in your head, self-generated beliefs that you may have formed because of past experiences or events that left a mark on how you think. However, the effect they can have on your life is very real. Blockers can hold you back. For example, you may have grown up being told by parents or teachers that you'll "never amount to anything," and you've internalized those words until they became your belief. There's no *real* reason for you to hold that belief, but it has been with you for so long that you've allowed it to define who you are. Your mind is a powerful tool, so whatever you believe, positive or negative, is what will be manifested in your reality. This means if you're focusing on a perceived blocker, it becomes impossible to move past it. The only way around or over a blocker is to realize that your blocker is not real.

To clear blockers, you must acknowledge your perceived blocker for what it really is: a perception. You have to walk through your belief and challenge yourself to see the reality of it and see how holding that belief is limiting you.

Potential blockers can be:

- Fear of the unknown
- Lack of stability; fear of moving away from a stable lifestyle or routine
- Fear of not being accepted
- Fear of not being successful
- Fear of being alone
- Fear of stepping out of the status quo
- Lack of resources; fear of not having what it takes—not enough money or a belief of being insignificant or that you're from the wrong side of the tracks

Ask yourself — "Am I holding on to a belief that is not based on anything real?"

For example, you might want to further your career in corporate America, but you also happen to be a very beautiful woman, and you believe you won't be taken seriously because of how you look. It's what you believe: if you believe in a blocker, it will come to pass. If you're fearful of being rejected, that's the frequency you send out, and you *will* be rejected. On the other hand, if you believe that you're not going to be rejected, even if you are then rejected, you won't see it as rejection, you'll just accept it as something that's not right for you or that the time is not right for you.

When you understand your soul purpose and accept your soul purpose, you also accept that the universe will provide everything you need to fulfill that purpose, and nothing—no person or thing— can get in your way. Blockers are the people or things that *you* believe are standing in your way, but they are self-limiting beliefs.

Blockers become voices in your head that are louder than any other little intuitive voices or voices of reason. Perhaps, someone told you often when you were younger that you were ugly, and it really hurt you. You internalized that voice and it became your belief, so later in life when another little voice is saying you're pretty and you're worthy, the voice of your blocker drowns it out. Blockers can take over and take control. When they take control, it becomes a self-perpetuated downward cycle. You believe that you're not worthy or that you're ugly, so you find things in your life to confirm that belief, and because you're looking for those things, your focus is only on the negative happenings in your life. Those negatives then become all you find. You continue to find the confirmation you're looking for, and in so doing, you continue to feed your blockers and give them more power—you make your belief your reality.

Take back control by reconnecting with your source of inspiration and empowering yourself by reconnecting with your gift and your soul purpose.

When I first entered corporate America, I was trying to figure out what my niche was, and I was unsure of how best to articulate who I was and what I had to offer. I had grown up reading books, so when I encountered this potential blocker, I went to the bookstore and bought a book on communication. By doing that, I realized just how many different levels of communication there are and how there are ways of communicating clearly for all different personality types. This information that helped me move forward, I could have defined as a blocker; however in this case I just needed direction. Gaining an understanding of how to communicate clearly without trying to be anything other than myself gave me the power to overcome my fear of going into an unknown environment. I had an inner confidence knowing that just being myself was all I needed to be.

Furthering your education is only one way of learning to overcome limiting beliefs. If it's your belief that you have to be an outgoing personality to get ahead in your profession, and you know yourself to be an introvert, you will allow your belief to hold you back. Your personality hasn't *really* prevented you from getting ahead, but your belief that it will hold you *has* held you back. Blockers might be internal or external, but really none of them are actual blocks. They are merely what you perceive to be blocks. The way to overcome them is to reprogram yourself, to change your thinking and clear the way forward mentally. There are a number of exercises that can be helpful, with one of the most effective being the use of positive affirmations.

> *"Here's the problem. Most people are thinking about what they don't want, and they're wondering why it shows up over and over again."*
> —John Assaraf

The best solution will depend on how huge you perceive your blocker to be and on what stage of life or of your business you're at. Overcoming *your* blockers becomes possible when you find something you can align yourself with, something positive that you can believe in to help you override long-held negative beliefs. Learning to believe in yourself is *the* most effective way to do this.

When blockers appear, I take the power from them. For example, when I worked in corporate America, positions as manager would become available, and I'd talk with my colleagues about the fact that there were no minority managers. As a member of a minority group, this could have been seen as a blocker, as could other beliefs such as being too young, but when presented with opportunities like that I'd think, *why not? Why shouldn't I go for it?* My thoughts were that the worst that could happen would be that I wouldn't get the job. I'd take the power from potential blockers by putting myself forward and presenting a strong case for my suitability for the position.

> *"Everyone needs something to believe in,*
> *and I believed in myself."*
> —Muhammad Ali

Positive affirmations are a powerful tool that can help you overcome blockers by drowning out the negative voice you hear in your mind. Blockers don't necessarily appear overnight, so you have become programmed over time to think in a certain way and to hold certain beliefs. Your beliefs have become habits, and you're not always aware of the fact that they are actually holding you back. It takes time to change your thinking and accept that you *can* change your thinking. Repeating positive affirmations is a way of establishing a new habit. Affirmations that are positive and supportive of you being your best self and of you living your soul purpose are a way of reprogramming your thought processes. When you're repeating them out loud and saying them with courage, you're standing in your purpose, and you're changing your beliefs.

When you know your true self, when you learn to recognize and accept your soul purpose, it becomes possible to detach yourself from limiting beliefs because you learn to accept and love who you *really* are, not who the voice of your blockers would have you believe you are.

There can be times when you know your purpose, and you take steps to implement your purposeful plan, but your limiting beliefs prevent you from living fully in your purpose or from being of the utmost service in your purpose. It may be that you're feeling uncomfortable with being paid to do something that comes so easily to you. It's possible that you might believe yourself to be a bad person because you make a lot of money or because you're taking money from people for something that is easy for you: You may be asking, "How can I possibly charge for this?"

Thinking this way creates blockers because you become someone who has so much to give to the universe and the people you're here to serve, but yet you will be in poverty because you're unable to accept the abundance that will come your way through being of service through your soul purpose. Your beliefs are preventing you from stepping into your soul purpose fully and accepting your abundance; you are undervaluing yourself and the gift you have to offer. You believe yourself to be not good enough or not worthy of being paid the amount you're paid, yet you'll struggle to see that it's those very beliefs that are preventing you from moving forward and getting to wherever it is you want to be. The first step toward clearing blockers is to accept that you have them.

Recognizing Blockers

Ask yourself — is this really true? Stand firm and really question the truthfulness of the statement you're making.

For example, if you're saying, "it's going to take too long to achieve this goal," you must question why you believe your statement to be true. Let's say you're 34 years old, and you don't have a bachelor's degree, but it's something you've always wanted to do. You know it's a goal that will take four years to accomplish, so your thoughts are that it's a goal that takes too long. You choose not to go for your goal because you know you'll be 38 years old before you achieve it, and you believe it'll be too late to do anything with it by then. Your belief is a limiting belief that is going to hold you back. However, if you change your thinking, you'll realize that you have every reason to go for your goal and no real reason at all not to go for it. If you don't go for it, four years will pass soon enough and you'll still be 38, but you won't have a bachelor's. Is four years really too long when you think of it that way? Truthfully, what are the benefits of not going for it and of not achieving your dream? When you question your belief, you realize that you have far more to lose by not doing it than you have by going ahead and doing it.

As another example, you may be holding back from going to a job interview by saying, "I'm too young; they're never going to hire me." Is that really true? Why do you believe they won't hire you? Is it really because of your age, or is it because you need some additional skills and experiences? When you question what's true, you find what your real blockers are, and you can then find ways to clear them. In this case, you can take positive steps to prepare yourself for the interview and get yourself in a position to be hired. Why not just go for it? If you don't go for the interview, you can't get hired. Blockers stop you from doing things. Your beliefs further feed your blockers, and the more you believe those blockers to be real, the more difficult it becomes to move past them. You become stuck.

For example, early in my career, I already had my master's of science in healthcare policy and administration from the Stetson School of Business and Economics at Mercer University. I graduated at a time when healthcare was changing rapidly, and due to the rapid change, I was just as qualified to obtain a Director's job at a start-up as an experienced person was, primarily because when I was studying in school, I was researching, writing, and studying the changes and implications of managed care in the U.S. and how healthcare was delivered differently across the world. I had studied the implications of change and how to best prepare organizations to successfully navigate the new terrain. While I was in school, I worked in healthcare. I could have *not* gone for the top jobs *or* gone for the Director's positions due to my age; however, I did not let that stop me. When I kept on moving, I discovered that based on my experience and skills, I was able to compete with professionals twice my age.

I had a client who was very young, and although he had not gone to college, he had always worked with technology. In high school he found a passion for technology and programming, and due to his passion and his consistent investment in himself, he had stayed current with programming languages. He thought that no one would employ him because of his age, but once we worked together, he realized that what he had been doing as a hobby was a hot commodity. He was able to present himself in a way that employers would understand what he had to offer. Initially, if you looked at his resume, it would appear that he had no experience, but when he was able to put his hobby projects, awards, and certifications on his resume, it was a totally different response from employers. He was able to gain employment with Fortune 500 companies successfully at the age of twenty, and he has not looked back since.

It's understandable to accept that your age may limit your potential to secure that particular position, but by going for it anyway, you move forward and other opportunities may well present themselves as a result of having put yourself forward for that position. The company may see the value you represent and offer you a different position, or it may refer you to another party who is looking to hire someone with your skills.

> *"To begin to think with purpose is to enter the ranks*
> *of those strong ones who only recognize failure*
> *as one of the pathways to attainment."*
> —James Allen

Everyone's blockers are different, and what one person sees as a blocker is not necessarily a blocker for someone else. I never saw being too young as a blocker; I always chose to just go for it anyway. If someone says, "You can't do that," I instantly question, "Why not?" You are who you are and your beliefs are your beliefs, but we all have the capacity to change our beliefs.

Early in my career, I believed that success and money equaled being alone. I had to question why I believed that to be true. I knew that if I were living my purpose, I would attract people into my life, so I had to turn that knowledge into a belief and trusted that I would be provided for; I had to believe that what I needed would be provided and that if I accepted my soul purpose, stood in that purpose, and used my gift to be of service in that purpose, I would attract the people I needed into my life at the right time. I reprogrammed myself to *believe* that by using affirmations, and it worked. I put out positive energy and received positive energy in return in the form of all the people from all over the world whom I met and continue to meet on a regular basis. I have grown in my purpose, and I have attracted so many wonderful people into my life. I'm not alone. If I'd given into my belief that abundance equaled being alone and allowed that belief to be a blocker, I would have missed out on so much.

You have to believe in yourself, and you have to be able to detach yourself from the opinion of others. Even dynamic, successful people who outwardly appear super confident can have blockers. Individuals can face moments of doubt when they find themselves questioning whether their gift is really all they need to be able to fulfill their purpose and if they really have what it takes to live their purpose fully. These doubts often stem from negative external sources, so the more grounded you become in who you really are, the easier it is to detach yourself from negative voices and stand firm in your soul purpose. *Your* beliefs set *your* energy, so it's important to remain positive and maintain your belief in yourself and your abilities. If you believe you're going to fail at something, you set that energy and a course of action that will create that reality.

> *"If you think you can do a thing or think*
> *you can't do a thing, you're right."*
> —Henry Ford

Letting Go of Blockers

Sometimes people hold on to blockers because they believe those blockers to have served them well in the past. For example, some might hold on to the belief that nobody loves them. Because they think that way, the people around them keep trying to show them that they *are* loved, but the long-held belief remains a blocker, and no matter what anyone says or does, it's never going to be enough to change their thinking. In fact, their blocker has become such a habit that they've become comfortable in that place in their mind. Changing their thinking would make them uncomfortable because if they let go of that blocker, would they get any attention at all?

Holding on to a blocker can also be a way of choosing not to have to do anything. When this is the case, someone will use their belief that something is not possible as a reason not even to bother trying. Or, a blocker could be used as a reason to give up on something.

218

If someone tries something and experiences a difficulty, they can use the blocker as a reason not to stick with it. When people face doubts, blockers can become "reasons" to stay still and not move, but those reasons are not real and there's no long-term benefit in hiding behind them. Blockers prevent you from living your purpose fully, so giving power to any form of blocker will not serve you in the long-run.

> *Focus on what you can do to move forward and*
> *achieve your goals, not what you can't do or don't have.*
> —Unknown

It's possible that you may recognize your blockers but choose to stay blocked by them simply because you're comfortable where you are. You're comfortable, but you're not fulfilled. There's a difference. It could be that you've gained a certain amount of status or recognition, and although you know you're not fulfilled, you don't want to move from where you are because you don't want to give up what you have. It's possible that you may even *create* blockers just to keep yourself where you are. You might tell yourself, "I won't make as much money;" "My wife wouldn't be happy with me if I started my own business;" "I won't be worthy of love if I'm not the bread winner;" or "What would my kids think?"

Blockers can be there, but it's how you deal with them that matters. Your blockers can only remain blockers if you feed them and allow them to take control of your thought processes. As you find a way through one blocker, another may appear further down the line, but the blockers themselves are never a problem when you continue to move forward and look for ways to work through them.

Some blockers may need professional help to get you to a point where you can move fully into living your soul purpose, but the most important thing is to always remain positive; always stay on a high frequency and focus on living in the moment. Worrying about things that have already happened and, therefore, can't be changed or things that haven't yet happened can only serve to keep you on a low frequency. Learning to think positively allows you to generate positive energy. Positive thoughts lead to positive actions, and positive actions lead to positive outcomes. You might not have all the answers, but you can choose to try to see where it takes you or you can choose to give up and stay exactly where you are— unfulfilled.

> *"You miss 100 percent of the shots you don't take."*
> —Wayne Gretzky

When I was in undergraduate school at Furman University, I volunteered at the Urban League. I was tutoring high school students who really didn't see the point of applying themselves. They believed there was no point because they knew they were not going to be able to afford to go to college anyway. It was only when they verbalized their belief that it became possible to help them change that belief by telling them about all the options that were available to them. They were unaware of the options they had, but by gaining a new understanding, the blocker they had been feeding with their belief was removed.

Recognize and acknowledge your blockers, but also acknowledge that those blockers are fed by your beliefs and you have the power to work through or around them by challenging your beliefs and recognizing the truth.

Clearing Blockers
Create your own positive affirmations, examples are: "I attract abundance" or "I attract joy." Say these things several times each day and repeat them several times over each time.

Question your blockers; ask yourself why you hold a certain belief, and answer truthfully.

Verbalize your blocker; say what you believe out loud and see how it sounds! Look at it for what it really is.

CHAPTER FIFTEEN
REVIEW AND REDEFINE

*"Goals are simply tools to focus your energy in positive directions.
These can be changed as your priorities change,
new ones added, and others dropped."*
—Unknown

ONCE YOU'RE LIVING YOUR SOUL purpose and monetizing it, it's always a good idea to keep checking on how things are progressing, which is something you should purposefully do on a regular basis. It's an opportunity to pause and take a look at what's working and what's not working, what's working with your style and what needs to be tweaked, and it provides an effective way of tracking your progress.

Pausing to review allows you to make appropriate adjustments, but it's important to keep on moving. A review might include checking the number of people you planned to speak to over a set period of time against the actual number you spoke to. You might also review the responses you received and look for areas where you see room for improvement. What could be better? What could you do to make your services the most attractive to your tribe; what could you do better to be of the utmost service to them?

It's an opportunity to reassess your purposeful plan. A review is a way of looking at your plan now that you're in it and now that you're actually doing what you planned to do. Not everything will always go according to the plan, so adjustments may be needed—and it's okay to readjust. Always stay open to making changes and be receptive to making changes that will help keep you on track to achieving your ultimate aim. When you're living your purpose and using your gift to be of service, you need to stay open to new ideas so that you continue making the most of what you have to offer and providing the best service to your tribe.

Don't stop. Keep on going.

Your tribe will evolve, and you will evolve. Never give up and never stop moving forward. When you do all of the things discussed in this book, you are well on your way, but it's an ongoing process. Touch base with yourself regularly and purposefully. Review your plan and, based on what you find, revise it. Is it really working for you? What's not working for you? Revise your purposeful plan so that you can best leverage your soul purpose and monetize it.

You may choose to have another expert eye help you track your progress, and you might seek recommendations, suggestions, and advice from other sources. This can be an effective way of keeping up with any new trends you should know about or that could help you. When evaluating the things that are not working out, it's important to consider whether you have committed to it for long enough to really see if it's working for you. For example, some kinds of marketing provide instant benefits, while other types of marketing provide benefits in the long-term. Your message has to be out there to reach your tribe and for them to act on it, so you have to look at the bigger picture and evaluate how every aspect of your plan is working overall.

Review your progress in terms of meeting the targets set out in your plan. If you're up against challenges all of the time, you may need to reset your targets. If you're in your first year of trading, you may be happy to break even, but if you're in your second year, you're expecting to see improvements on your first year achievements. Your first year might not be your most profitable year, but you're planting the seed, and in your second year, you can cash in on all the hard work you've already put in. In the second year, you're leveraging what you've done in the first year, so you're looking to raise more revenue. In the third year, you can reap the rewards of all the systems you now have in place, and all of your time can now be focused on providing your service and being the best you can be. It's all about being fulfilled and living your soul purpose.

Often, it can take a business up to five years or more to obtain the maximum strides. There are always opportunities to improve and support your vision of success. Even with larger corporations implementing big changes and taking on large new initiatives to improve their business, it takes about two to three years to gain the maximum benefits of the change and be able to measure the improvements the change has made. Continually identify ways that can help you better monetize your soul purpose by being able to leverage your offerings and gifts in the best way possible.

The greatest success is being yourself.

There is no conclusion here. There is just an invitation.

Here is to your abundant life.

"Imagine what a harmonious world it could be if every single person, both young and old, shared a little of what he is good at doing."
—Quincy Jones

"If the human race wishes to have a prolonged and indefinite period of material prosperity, they have only got to behave in a peaceful and helpful way toward one another."
—Winston Churchill

"An essential part of a happy, healthy life is being of service to others."
—Sue Pattom Thoele

"Everybody can be great. Because anybody can serve. You only need a heart full of grace. A soul generated by love."
—Martin Luther King, Jr.

"Our greatest duty and our main responsibility is to help others. But please, if you can't help them, would you please not hurt them."
—Dalai Lama

"When you help someone up a hill, you find yourself closer to the top."
—Brownie Wise

Abundance — Overflow – Prosperity – Affluence – Plentiful – Wealth – Abundance – Overflow – Prosperity – Affluence – Plentiful – Wealth – Abundance

I hope this book was helpful for those readers who needed to be reminded that they already had all the gifts they needed in order to be of service and live a very prosperous life. I hope I've been able to show you not only how you can identify your soul purpose in life and monetize it, but also examples of people who have already done it. I want to encourage you to step out courageously. When you accept yourself, good things will happen. For both businesses and individuals, when your focus is serving your tribe and your community in the best way, you will not go wrong. There's money to be made in living your soul purpose. This world is full of abundance. Living your soul purpose and being of the utmost service is an opening to a new world to those who give of their gifts to those who need them most. The world is full of abundance for those of us who accept the value that we bring in all we do and understand our worth and our fingerprint.

Abundance — Overflow – Prosperity – Affluence – Plentiful – Wealth – Abundance – Overflow – Prosperity – Affluence – Plentiful – Wealth – Abundance

ABOUT
THE AUTHOR

Melissa Evans, MHA, PMP, Master Coach, self-made millionaire by 31 and "The Guru of Implementation," founded The Broshe Group in 2001 in Atlanta, Georgia. She has a track record of both making money AND helping others make money while remaining true to themselves.

Under Evans' dynamic leadership, The Broshe Group has established itself as a transformational force, enhancing people's professional and personal lives. Unlike other companies, The Broshe Group guarantees clients a return on their investment if they closely follow its proven formulas and strategies for generating profits. Currently based in Atlanta, Georgia, U.S.A., Detroit, Michigan, U.S.A and Toronto, Ontario, Canada, The Broshe Group is a privately-held firm that serves businesses worldwide.

Ready to Attract Massive Abundance Into Your Life AND Live Your Soul Purpose?

Introducing the Sole to Soul Digital Workbook...
Yours FREE for a Limited Time

This workbook is the perfect companion to the powerful and life-changing lessons you've been reading in *Sole to Soul*. Just go to **SoletoSoulBook.com** for an instant download. You'll get all the tools, worksheets, and everything that you need to fully integrate the teachings of this book, so you can live your life to its FULLEST—attracting all the abundance you've dreamed of while living your soul purpose.

This workbook (valued at $24.95) is my gift to you as someone who has invested in themselves by reading this book. Here's that link again to get your instant download: **SoletoSoulBook.com**.

PRAISE FOR MELISSA EVANS AND THE BROSHE GROUP

"A vision without an implementation plan is useless. Melissa will show you how to create systems and consistently implement your plan. She will teach you how to carry your vision through to goals and action plans. If you want to implement, talk to Melissa."

— Donna Price, Rose Compass Consulting

"I have consulted with Melissa Evans on a weekly basis to get coaching and have implemented what she teaches. When it comes to business training and entrepreneurial coaching, consult with Melissa. You won't be sorry."

— Kiki Ramsey, Kiki Ramsey International

"I am so impressed by Melissa Evans, the Guru of Implementation. You may have great ideas, but you need to know how to implement them. She will show you how to take action."

— Hueina Su, The Nurturer's Coach

"I really enjoy working with you and the energy and excitement and professionalism you bring to our company, consultants, and clients."

— Matt Tant, President, HCTec

"Melissa was the first person from McKesson I met when I came to the hospital six months ago. At the time I was feeling like I had grabbed on to a bullet train moving at 150 miles an hour! She came to my office and volunteered to help me understand the timeline and scope of all the safety stack projects. I remember being so impressed with her total recall of the most minute details and the logical and organized way her mind worked as she progressed through a verbal description of the projects.

In a recent presentation to a leadership group, I mentioned that I believed the keys to being successful with these projects was relentless planning and a good team working on all facets of the plan. Melissa had been instrumental in both areas. Her planning skills, along with the incredible tools McKesson has put together to shepherd and manage the projects, made me feel as though there was a steady hand guiding the projects through all of the potential pitfalls."

— Michael J. Melby, MS, BCPS, Director of Pharmacy,
Bloomington Hospital

INTERNATIONAL PRAISE FOR SOLE TO SOUL

"I was inspired to move into action, to create my own 'fingerprint' as Melissa suggests. The concept is so relatable. Unifying one's soul and sole purpose is paramount to spiritual and financial growth and achievement. Each chapter is laden with helpful tips for business and life in general..."

— Tricia Allen, Analyst, Bombardier Aerospace, Toronto, Canada

"A powerful tool designed to empower anyone who is seeking self-improvement and increase self-esteem. It provides practical, easy to understand principles that can be applied by any person."

— Redinela Mani, PMP, Project Coordinator, Cancer Care Ontario, Canada

"As a spiritual arts therapist, I so much appreciate inspiration through graspable metaphors full of rich imagery. Just after reading some chapters from *Sole to Soul,* insights flowed through me, such as the vitality of our own fingerprint uniqueness, something that each of us have! This brings me such a deep sense of peace and added validation of my own uniqueness. I am touched with similar insights that I will now weave into my life as rich and practical soul nectar. Thank you Melissa for this creation! I couldn't recommend *Sole to Soul* enough!"

— Daniella Rubinovitz, Visual Dialogue Mentor, Amsterdam, DaniellaRubinovitz.com

"A great book to help you, make YOU your most valuable asset."

— Gent Asllani, Graphic Designer, Tower Litho, Canada

"If you are unclear about what your true purpose is for either yourself or your business, then *Sole to Soul* is a must-read for you. Melissa Evans has a talent for showing how to tap into your soul purpose in a way that is easy to understand and implement."

—Karin Volo, President, Inspiring Your Very Best, Inc.,Sweden